POSTCARD MARKETING

IN AN ONLINE WORLD

A COMPLETE GUIDE TO MARKETING WITH POSTCARDS
HOW TO TARGET ONLY THOSE MOST LIKELY TO BUY FROM YOUR BUSINESS
12 POINT DESIGN TEST THAT 75% OF MAIL PIECES FAIL
INTEGRATING EMAIL AND ONLINE MARKETING FOR BETTER RESULTS

JOY GENDUSA

FOUNDER OF POSTCARDMANIA, PCMDIGITAL, ROCKET PRINT & MAIL

Disclaimer
I hate to add this disclaimer, but the lawyers said that I have to. Despite the fact that you read this book and do exactly what I say to do — if you do not get the results you thought you would, it is not my responsibility. In other words, you read and apply this book at your own risk. All of it has worked for my business and the businesses of thousands of my clients. But it may not work for you.

Acknowledgments

This book is a collaboration. It would not have come together if not for many hardworking, dedicated individuals.

Thank you: Joe Niewerski for being brilliant and helping me write, Sarah Kicinski for keeping me organized and also for being brilliant and Jessica Lalau — you are a star — just so, so good! I'd also like to acknowledge the following people for their help:

Shannon Johnson
Melissa Bradshaw
Shaun Metzger
Matthew Alenduff

Table of Contents

Section 4: Campaigning and Tracking

Section 5: Different Industries and What Works for Them

Section 6: Glossary

INTRODUCTION
POSTCARDS FROM THE EDGE

---

*"Marketing is not an event, but a process...
It has a beginning, a middle, but never an end, for it is a
process. You improve it, perfect it, change it, even pause it.
But you never stop it completely."*
– Jay Conrad Levinson

Picture yourself in a grocery store, eager to get in and out in twenty minutes or less. Now imagine yourself with a cart full of bread, milk and eggs, rushing toward the checkout aisles. But wait, they're all full; all except one.

Is it a mirage, a trick, a hoax? Nope; it's for real. Its light is on, a cashier stands patiently behind her register beckoning you over with a smile and a wave, and yet everyone remains in some other, crowded line. What do you do? Take up the last spot in one of the other nine full-to-bursting lines or saunter over and march right up to the empty line?

That's what I thought you'd say. Well, in the world of modern marketing, there is a secret checkout aisle just waiting to beckon you over with a smile and a wave. It's no hoax, no mirage, and it works like nothing else you've ever tried before.

It may not have a lot of bells or whistles or fancy new gadgets to recommend it, you may not see it on the cover of some glossy ad agency magazine, but like that empty grocery store aisle it's out there, ready and waiting for you to rediscover the leverage, opportunity and possibility that exists by turning left when everybody else is going right. It's called postcard marketing and before you call it old-fashioned and dated, give it a second look. Truthfully, there are some new bells and whistles, but we'll get to those in Chapter 19.

Let's go back to our grocery store analogy. That empty aisle that looked so inviting is the road less traveled, the path everyone's forgotten about, or maybe even gone down already and didn't find success so they doubled-back to follow the herd into one of the other aisles.

Those other aisles? They are all those *"other"* marketing tactics that everybody else is busy beating into the ground. I'm not saying they don't work — some of them work quite well, given the right company, needs and circumstances. But wouldn't you rather be a stand-out, using a direct-marketing tool often overlooked by your competitors, than send out, email, SPAM or blitz prospects with the same blind items everybody else is using?

Yup, I thought perhaps you'd say that, too. I feel that my first duty in this manual is to convince you beyond any doubt that postcards, as your direct mail marketing tool, are the absolute BEST path to follow. In this brief introduction, I'm going to spend the next few pages trying to do just that. Along the way, I'll give you my own experiences succeeding with postcards and I'll share with you the case studies of others winning with them, too.

There are doubters who will say, *"Why should I believe you? If I believe what you say and market with postcards, you stand to profit from my expenditure — you may just be writing all of this for that!"*

Let's face facts. It is true that I own a postcard marketing company — the biggest and fastest growing one in the USA. It is true that I hope to win your business by sharing my expertise on this subject. However, just because I have a vested interest in your marketing with postcards does not mean that it doesn't work. And, just because I may stand to profit if you jump on the postcard marketing bandwagon it does not mean that I'm not offering the best service and product for the money at my company, PostcardMania. Heck, you could take all my advice and go elsewhere if you want! That's right; postcards work whether my company produces them for you or somebody else does!

You can choose to believe me or not. I am writing this manual after being in the postcard business for more than 24 years. I started with an idea and I used ONLY postcards for the first few years to promote my business. At the time of this writing, we are a staff of over 330 employees strong and we did over 83 million dollars in earnings last year. Over and over again, friends and colleagues asked me how I did it.

Now is my chance to tell them, to tell you and to tell anybody else who'll listen just exactly how I did it. In this manual, I am speaking from experience and not only my own experience — but that of countless others. (Well, not countless. We have over 100,000 extremely satisfied customers with more coming on board every day.)

Along the way, I've spent time and energy culling the successful actions of several different industries — all using this particular direct mail technique — the postcard. I have learned how to get results, plain and simple. I have already taught all of this to my staff. Here I will share that with you.

I know that I can teach you EXACTLY how to succeed with postcard marketing. I know it completely and utterly. I also know that, if done correctly, when you find your particular *"formula"* for your own business — and if you stick to it — you will, without a doubt, have terrific success.

What is terrific success?

Well, that all depends on what you want to achieve. Some of our clients want merely to spread the word of a new gym opening in the neighborhood; others want to send an announcement to the entire Southwest. For them, five gym members — or 500 new clients — might spell *T-E-R-R-I-F-I-C*.

What about you?

In this book, I will share with you specific postcard designs that have produced proven results for a variety of very different, but profitable, industries. From dentists to day spas, from attorneys to art galleries, from real estate agents to restaurants, we've custom designed campaigns to meet every client's specific needs. If you don't find your industry in this book or online, don't fret; I will go out of my way to find you a sample if you email me directly: joy.gendusa@postcardmania.com. But even better than that, I'll show you how to figure out what headline — and what image — will create the kind of results you're looking for.

Once you've got your headline and image, though, don't stop there; there is so much more to successful marketing with postcards than the headline and the image. Please read the manual in its entirety. You will not regret it. At the very least, it will validate what you already know. On the other end of the spectrum, you will come away with an easily executable plan that will help you increase your bottom line by just as much — or as little — as you want to.

I suggest you keep a pen and pad in hand while reading this. I'm sure you'll be coming up with all kinds of bright ideas for your own company — or the company you work for. If you don't have a pad handy when a brilliant idea strikes, feel free to write in the liberal margins provided or go to town with different colored markers or highlighter pens to pinpoint your favorite quote, tip or factoid. Yes, unlike your junior high history teacher, I encourage you to write in this book!

Opportunity, ideas and potential brilliance are simply too important to limit to just the margins. Speaking of limits, there really are no limits to how far you can go and I'll show you how direct mail marketing with postcards will get you there. (Wherever *"there"* is for you and your specific needs.)

My story in a nutshell: I started PostcardMania in June of 1998. I started it as a pilot program — a test. My business back then — before PostcardMania.com — was called Joy Rockwell Enterprises and I was a four-person agency specializing in the design and printing of business collateral (any printed matter for the business — brochures, info packs, pocket folders, etc.).

I was in business for four years up to that point. I was definitely struggling. My boys were only tykes then and I had to work around the clock to make a decent living. I desperately wanted to change my business so that I could spend more time with my kids, but still expand my company.

Even though I always recommended to my clients to engage in plenty of direct mail, I wasn't following my own advice. I NEVER mailed out anything — except invoices! What a hypocrite I was!

At that time most of my business was from one very big client. And to make a long and horrible story short and sweet — they went down for unethical business practices and I could see the end coming for me. That is, if I didn't do something to attract more clients — and quick!

They say that necessity is the mother of invention, and they're right; this was the impetus I needed to heed my own advice and do a mailing of my own. As an industry *"insider"* I received mailings from all kinds of different printing companies because I was a *"reseller"* for them. One day I got a postcard from a postcard company. It was fantastic. I could get 5,000 postcards for $425!! Back then, this was UNHEARD OF. Needless to say, I called immediately.

I did eventually get my postcards. But, the process was aggravating, to say the least. The customer service was appalling. They weren't friendly and didn't seem to give a hoot if I was happy or not. And, frankly, the paper they used was thin and the ink smudged when it went through mail machines at the post office.

What's that saying about God closing one door and opening a window? My thought at the time was: I could do this same thing WAY better, and charge less, and create a *"higher end"* product and be nice to the people that call me just by caring about their order and their results!

At this point, I could say, *"The rest is history!"* But I'll be more honest than that. It was scary, rough-going and treacherous and many, many times I wanted to quit. Creating a business from nothing is more than a big task and not everyone is cut out for it. Plenty of times I feared I wasn't either.

How was I going to get enough new business to feed my family, pay my staff and all the bills? Often I thought that I'd done everything I possibly could and it still felt like we'd take two steps forward and one step back — or three steps back. Oh, how frustrated I was. And I was still working 12 hours a day, 7 days a week.

More time with my kids?

Yeah, right!

What SAVED MY BUSINESS??? (I wanted to write that last sentence like this: WHAT SAVED MY LIFE? — but it sounded too dramatic. Seriously, though, something very specific did save my business and thus my life.) It's too simple, but it's the truth. And the answer is: mailing out postcards every single week to promote what we sell — postcards. And let me repeat something: EVERY SINGLE WEEK, in 24 years, we've never missed a week — not even during the 2008 recession or the COVID-19 craziness.

The hardest part was figuring out how much mail I needed to send out in order to make enough income to be profitable. This was a very tricky formula when designed from scratch, with no road map in place, but rest assured there is a chapter in this manual (Chapter 21) devoted to that so that it will be easier for you than it was for me.

In that particular chapter, I cover figuring out the correct estimation of effort required to succeed with direct mail. (If only I had such a chapter when I was starting out!) Instead, I definitely learned by trial and error. I figured out a formula to get close to the right amount of effort. By effort I'm referring to *"how much money should I spend?"* and *"how much mail should I send?"* and *"how often should I do a mailing?"* I say *"formula,"* but there is no pat answer; it's going to be different for different industries that all have different margins.

The beautiful part about what I do is that I get to deal with so many (over 350) different industries. I've learned what works for many of these and I plan to tell you stories of success from quite a few in this manual — in addition to sharing several case studies and images of the cards that are working!

When I realized that I had to mail out postcards each and every week, I started with 1,000 pieces per week and I hit a general business list based on geography. Not super smart, granted, but super easy. I bought a yellow pages CD (remember those?) and mailed to my local area.

Later we changed the mailings to go to specific industries.

As my efforts were rewarded with business, I increased to 2,500 pieces per week.

Twenty-four plus years later, we mail 180,000 pieces per week just to promote us!

Over this period of time, I not only spent a small fortune on my *"trial and error"* learning method — which you will now be able to avoid — I also spent thousands of hours researching, learning and compiling what really works and what doesn't. None of this is theory. It's truly based on my hard-won experiences — my own and those of my customers. So it doesn't have to take you nearly 24 years to get your business to grow to where mine is. You can do it faster and smarter! I've seen lots of my clients do just that!

I hope you feel inspired. I hope you are still interested. I hope you keep reading and I hope you implement what you learn. Of course, what I hope for you is insignificant compared to what you must hope for yourself.

Remember: *Nothing but your own experience will really convince you.*

That's just my opinion, but I've seen it time and time again with my customers. They cross their fingers and blindly trust us — hoping they're not throwing their money away. Honestly, the folks that stick with it never stop coming back for more. Why? Because it works. And they're winning with their marketing efforts — in a big way. In fact, one of our top clients made the *Inc. 500 List* — one year after we did — for being one of the fastest-growing, privately-held companies in the nation!

Now they know what I've known for years, and what you'll soon find out: direct mail postcards work!

◆ **Important Note:**

Every so often you will see a passage with this ◆ next to it. This will indicate to you that this particular piece of advice is very important and made a HUGE impact on my business when I implemented it. Now, have fun! I'm genuinely excited for you to start this adventure and change your business forever.

SECTION 1
WHY POSTCARDS?

In this section you will learn:

- Why marketing is essential to the health and growth of your business
- How direct mail postcards fulfill the requirements of marketing for your business
- Why postcards balance cost-efficiency and effectiveness better than any other marketing strategy available

1

MARKETING STRATEGY 101

———

Too often we skip past things — like titles — and nod our heads, assuming we know what they mean or even how they're defined. But let's slow down.

The term *"marketing strategy"* might sound broad or vague to many, so let's take the mystery out of it. Then you can understand, devise and implement your own marketing strategy — one that fits into your business plan.

Strategy comes from a Greek word *stratagein*, meaning to be a general. Think of a strategy as an overall plan of action needed to win a war. Smaller, detailed actions are called tactics. You can have tactical plans, which help you achieve your overall marketing strategy. That's simple enough, isn't it?

A marketing strategy is an overall plan of marketing actions you intend to take in order to accomplish a specific goal for your company.

Start with a goal: $2 million in sales this year, expand into new premises by a certain date, double the size of the company in two years — whatever that goal is for you, write it down, scratch it out, erase, fine tune — be specific. Make it something realistic, but challenging.

After you determine your goal, work out a simple, overall plan of the major marketing steps needed to accomplish that goal. Again, be specific. For example:

- Publish a newsletter for all existing customers and mail them out quarterly.
- Work out four special offers for the year and promote them to all your customers.
- Set up an e-commerce site and expand your website.
- Design a direct mail campaign promoting your website to all customers and prospects.
- Get mailing lists (of target markets), do a series of 12 postcard mailings, follow up and close all leads.

You get the idea. Take your time and really do your homework here. What worked in the past? Read up on successful marketing campaigns; talk to colleagues, friends and mentors. Don't be afraid to ask questions and play devil's advocate with your plan.

I always say marketing strategies are like blind dates — you don't have to be married to them. Pick and choose strategies that work best for you, based on analysis of past efforts — both yours and your competitors'.

◆ Do thorough research into your competition. Get on their mailing list and their email list, receive their promotions and discover what they do well and not so well. Then pick and choose those that will work best for you.

You don't need to reinvent the wheel. Being innovative is great, but doing what is already successful is practical and yields faster, more predictable results. Don't plagiarize anyone, but find out what offers make you want to call. Those will likely make others want to call, too. Research ALL your competition and take the best aspects of their marketing to come up with something original.

Your marketing strategy needs to be laid out in the right sequence and you should have some idea of a budget when you write it. Again, be realistic. *"Run a series of three, thirty-second TV ads during the Super Bowl"* might sound like a brilliant marketing strategy, but at five million dollars for each spot, can you really afford it?

Probably not.

On the other hand, when you build your marketing strategy, you can't cut corners. Save money where you can, but don't sacrifice quality for cost. Some things — like a great graphic designer or new technology to make mailings easier — are simply going to cost money. The payoff is reaching more people with more quality. If you don't promote heavily, it doesn't matter how good your product or service is, no one will know about it and you will go broke.

It can seem intimidating at first, I know, but don't worry. You are going to learn a lot in this manual and I will provide enough examples for you so you can figure out what the proper sequence is for your business.

Email <u>info@postcardmania.com</u> if you'd like to see a sample marketing program.

TWO-STEP MARKETING

When it comes to marketing your products or services, there are two basic challenges:

1.   How do you obtain new customers or clients? (By survey, this is the biggest concern for small businesses.)

2.   How do you get your existing customers to come back for more? This is not given nearly the importance it deserves by small business owners.

The direct mail postcard, when used correctly, answers both of these challenges admirably.

Nike® hit a popular slogan when they coined the phrase, *"Just Do It.™"* But in direct mail, we use a slightly more effective expression, *"Do It Right."* The difference between just doing it and doing it right is the difference between going through the motions and your sales going through the roof!

For example, the other day I received a postcard advertising computer monitors. It had teeny, tiny lettering slathered all over the front and a large portion of the back of the card. It was extremely hard to read, and what I could make out was very technical and jargon-y. As a result, I threw it away.

Several days later, I received a postcard with just 32 words on it. It quickly informed me that an auto detailer with a 4.8-star rating on Google (out of 200+ reviews) would be in my area every Saturday and Sunday offering full auto detailing for $50 for new customers who booked by calling his local phone number. How did I respond? I called. I asked about their openings, had my questions answered and booked a slot that Saturday for a full detail at 10 a.m.

What was the difference in my two responses? Why did one card go in the trash and another in the to-do pile? The auto detailing business used a time-tested, two-step selling process:

Step 1: Generate a lead. In the above example, getting me to call. Step 2: Provide the requested information.

Step two was provided to me on the phone by someone on their team, who answered my questions and made me feel confident that the service would be as good or better as my current one.

Why Exactly Does Two-Step Marketing Work?

A process that involves two steps allows a person to get comfortable before plunking down their hard-earned cash. Think about it, and you'll find most of life's biggest moments come in two stages. Like getting married or having a child, there is usually a *"warming up"* period to smooth the transition into the next stage.

Likewise, postcard marketing has two steps: step one is generating a lead; step two is providing the requested information. It is much easier to create interest (a lead) than walk a person through an entire buying process (a sale) on the first contact.

First, you execute step one, using postcards to inexpensively promote and target prospects and customers to generate leads (inquiries about your products and services). Then initiate step two when the prospect calls in and provides the requested information. By doing this, you convert the prospect into a sale.

This two-step process also helps you create a list of people who were interested enough to contact you. You can then re-contact the ones who didn't complete a sale when they first inquired, preferably until they do buy from you.

◆ IMPORTANT: Be sure to get the information you will need to re-contact the people who responded to your postcard offering. Repetitive follow-up with people who contact you will result in increased sales. Make it a company policy to follow up with those who contact you about your products and services.

The Most Effective Use of Postcards:
Generating Interest

The purpose of your postcard's message is to generate a sufficient level of interest in the mind of your prospect. All you want to do is get them to contact you about your offer. It may seem like an extra, *"padded"* step, but remember: you are generating interest, not collecting their money. (Not yet, anyway). That is what the two-step marketing process is about: Generating interested prospects and customers who contact you for more information.

Two-step marketing can even be expanded to three- or four-step marketing. Nowadays, folks can (and often prefer to) do all their due diligence online. They don't have to call you to get the information they now want from your postcard. So how do you generate that lead if they don't call you? You've got to entice them to fill out a form on your website at the very least.

This is what happens these days:

0. They get your postcard.
1. They go online, check out your website, and decide instantly whether they like you or not. (You know you've done that — gone to a site and instantly said to yourself, *"I like this site!"* or, *"I'm out of here."*) Regardless of how great your offer is, they could be gone in a flash. So now, step one is sending them someplace you know they'll feel comfortable. Yes, your site has to be that ultimate destination — a site that feels familiar somehow and embraces their personal aesthetic while caressing their innate sense of wholeness. Okay... I'm being a little facetious here, but I think you get the point. In order for them to even progress to step two, they have to like your website. They have to feel good there. They have to feel comfortable hanging out there, because you want them to spend enough time there to feel comfortable to get to the next step...

2. If they make it through step one, you now have to have an offer so good that they are willing to either call you or fill out a form on your website. There is this odd behavior amongst us humanoids... We perceive the danger of filling out an online form to be far greater than it is in reality. Worst-case scenario, you'll be contacted by a sales person — whhooooaaaa that's scary!! So getting folks to fill out your form is no easy feat, hence you need a great offer to motivate them.

In this system, step one is all about enticing them enough with your postcard to get them to type in your URL or scan your QR code. Step two is about generating that lead, aka filling out your form OR — if they really get that warm fuzzy feeling at your site — picking up the phone and calling you.

Now, when crafting your message, there are three necessary points to include:
1. The biggest benefit of your product or service: In the auto detailing example, it was cost savings.
2. A good reason for them to act NOW: some kind of *"special offer"* or deadline.
3. A simple, easy way for them to respond: your phone number, your website or an email address — or all three.

When it comes to postcard marketing, writing a bad message (or the wrong message) can be just as bad as writing no message at all. Your message should be short and to the point. Short messages on postcards produce more leads. For example, after clearly outlining your product's benefit, give a short call to action including something like this:

Call 1-800-628-1804 for Your Copy of Our Free Report.
If they call, you know they're interested.

Offer ends 05-05-22.
Print a date three weeks from your mailing date to create some urgency.

Lots of people will respond to find out what they might not know. Don't forget — they responded, which at least expresses some interest in the information you have created curiosity about. This method works and is sure to produce a large number of inquiries if sent to your proper market, which I'll explain how to define later in the manual.

Another two-step idea that works brilliantly for us is to place a website or landing page on the postcard and send the recipients to the page for something FREE, but valuable (our best offer is simply free samples of our products). When they go to the website, there is a fill-in section to capture their contact information in exchange for the free samples. These leads, for us, are a bit colder than someone that calls us — but now we can *"warm them up"* with more promotion.

This process will generate a bunch of leads from people who are truly interested in your products and services.

Why?

Because two-step marketing is based on proven buying behavior! Think about yourself and the way you make a buying decision.

3

POSTCARDS GET YOU NOTICED

When we got old enough to go to school, one of the first lessons we learned was NOT to draw attention to ourselves. We were taught a variety of ways to ensure we didn't stand out in a crowd. Don't slouch. Stand up straight. Use your inside voice. Smile for the camera. Wear what's in style.

Well, it's time to unlearn what we've been taught about standing out. In postcard marketing, it's all about standing out. It's all about getting what your kindergarten teacher preached against when you were six: **ATTENTION**!

I said earlier, my first order of business was to convince you why you should use postcards. Simply put, they're a great way to get attention. In this chapter, I'll show you how postcards get attention better than a standard direct mail piece. It may sound obvious, but there is more to it than meets the eye.

First, it is vital to understand that most people are bombarded with promotional jabber. They watch TV, they drive and see billboards, they get spammed — and they get those annoying pop-up messages or ads before videos when surfing the web.

You can probably think of a ton of other ways advertising reaches you, but you get my point. The bottom line is, anyone trying to market something in today's climate of *"promotional overload"* is at a distinct disadvantage. So, how do postcards break through and grab a prospect's attention?

First, they ditch the envelopes!

Truthfully, the most common question I am asked is, *"How do I get my prospect's attention?"*

This is a major problem because, no matter what you do to them, most envelopes look basically the same. Print them in color, make a window, stamp them URGENT — your customers have seen all these tricks before. They get thrown away before they're even opened.

Recipients can tell from the outside that it is a sales pitch, so they just toss it. This causes you to lose sales (and waste marketing dollars) due to assumptions made before your message is even read. If you had gotten the chance to show the prospect what you were offering, they might have gone for it.

The easiest way to get around this is by using postcards.

Second, people are relaxed and ready for your message when

they get your postcard and not only does the full-color aspect of postcards attract more attention than any envelope in a given day's stack of mail, it also allows you to deliver your message while recipients are deciding what to read and what to toss.

Let me paint a picture of this for you...

All day long you're checking and answering emails and deleting the ones that are a distraction because you're working. Those distracting emails are usually promoting something to you, right? But when you get your mail from your mailbox it's because you are ready for it. When you go through your pile of mail it's on YOUR terms — you have decided to look and either toss the mail or keep it for later.

While they're scanning the postcard to decide its fate, they're actually receiving your marketing message. This way, even if they do get rid of it (and most people will), they have already gotten the message. That lays the groundwork for future postcards (or online follow up ads — we'll get to that in Chapter 20).

Still not convinced? Let's use this example: you are sitting on the subway and the guy next to you leans over and says, *"I have something I would like to sell you. It's here under my trench coat. You interested?"*

As any sane person would, you move as far away from him as you can get.

Now, as you sit far removed from the untrustworthy freak in the trench coat, you are approached by a smiling little Girl Scout who holds out a box of cookies and says, *"Would you like to buy a box of cookies? Everyone loves the Thin-Mints!"*

As most sane people do, you pull out your wallet and plunk down $5 for a box of the delicious-yet-hardly-nutritious treats.

See the difference? The *"untrustworthy freak,"* as I have affectionately named him, could have actually had a box of Thin-Mints under there — but you weren't about to find out.

Don't hide your message behind a trench coat. Or should I say, stop stuffing your promo into envelopes!

THE POSTCARD ANSWER

I've explained why it is important to have a first *"warm up"* step incorporated into your marketing plan. And I have pointed out that postcards are a great way to get attention. Now it is time to explain why attention translates into a successful step one.

It is a time-tested truth in marketing that regular, repeated mailings are the way to create big, predictable results. When you mail every week or every month for a year, you will cause a dramatic growth in your business.

People respond to repetition. If you are a parent, you know how hard it is to refuse repeated requests for a cookie or a desperately wanted toy. If you are not a parent, I'm sure you remember asking, even begging for a toy, treat or permission to stay up past your bedtime until your parents finally gave in. Your customers and prospective customers respond the same way.

They need to be asked repeatedly.

There are really only four reasons people don't buy your products and services. In this chapter, we will discover what those reasons are, and how direct mail postcards overcome them.

Why someone doesn't buy something (and you can see this in your own buying behavior), is for one or more of these reasons:

- **No need**
- **No money**
- **No hurry**
- **No trust**

Now, let's go deeper.

- **No Need**

Don't take it so personally. Sometimes when people don't buy from you, it's because they simply don't want what you are offering. They may need what you are offering and not know or acknowledge that need, but the bottom line is they don't want it.

Yet.

Go where people want you. Avoid the square-peg-in-round-hole conundrum and look for a square hole. If you were dating, you wouldn't go hunting for a mate at a weekend retreat for newlyweds, would you? So why would you send your postcards to audiences that aren't interested in what you've got to offer?

Save lots of time, effort and money by targeting your postcard mailings to groups of people who have demonstrated they want your product or service — or ones similar to yours. If you follow this one piece of advice, you will become more profitable immediately.

Examples of those who have demonstrated they want your products and services are:
- Your own customers
- Your competitors' customers
- People who have purchased products and services that complement your products and services

Promotional mailings without a targeted market in mind aren't called postcards, they're called lottery tickets — and are about as effective as them.

Promote your business exclusively to people likely to respond to the benefits provided by your product or service.

- **No Money**

Businesses and consumers generally don't avoid purchases because they don't have the money necessary to purchase. They usually don't buy because they decide buying something else (like food) is more important to them.

You can get them to buy from you by making it clear buying your product or service will:
1) Get rid of something they don't want,
2) Get them something they do want, or
3) Get them more of something they already like.

It is your job to get people and businesses to understand that your products and services give them what they really want.

What is the most nagging problem you can solve for prospects in your targeted market?

Make sure they really feel what it will be like to have that problem eliminated. Use postcards to communicate how you can solve their problems. Later in the book, I'll show you lots of examples!

- **No Hurry**

People tend to drag their feet even after deciding to buy something. The longer they wait to purchase, the more likely they are to forget why your product or service is valuable or even necessary to them. Keep your message in front of them with repetitive mailings.

If you don't, you'll lose the business.

The reason repetitive mailings are so effective is that they remind your customers and prospects what they would be missing by not having your product or service. You can avoid losing sales because of *"no hurry"* by rewarding customers who take immediate action and penalizing those who don't. For example, offer a discounted price or a special bonus for ordering before a deadline. Then they will have a reason to hurry.

Mailing repetitively to targeted customers and prospects will close more sales.

Also, it is important to understand that the more expensive or complicated your product or service is, the more times you will have to hit them with your message before they will respond. A perfect example is a financial advisor. People rarely take action after seeing a postcard one time for this because it's a BIG decision.

- **No Trust**

Buyer's remorse is more than a clever buzz-word or catchphrase — it's a real problem losing us money as we speak. For most people, the fear of losing out is stronger than the desire to get something that could benefit them. This is instinctual self-protection. Unfortunately, it often causes people to avoid buying something they truly want or need.

I've been there. Have you?

When it comes down to it, nobody wants to buy something only to find out it won't solve his or her problem. They don't want to be (or even feel) ripped off, or still at a loss to the solution of their problem.

This is what you need to do to sidestep that reaction:
- Take away their risk in doing business with you
- Provide a way that they can trust you
- Remove any perceived risk

Here are three ways to build trust that I've found effective for any business:
1. Eliminate the risk with some kind of guarantee, such as a free trial, a money back guarantee or a *"keep the free gift even if you don't keep the product"* type of offer.
2. Give them testimonials from satisfied customers and/or provide references that prove the quality and reliability of your product or service.
3. Make it easy for your prospects and customers to

communicate with you and get their questions and concerns answered. Let them see that you and your business are real and you value earning and keeping their trust.

Give something to them BEFORE taking their money — and also after. For instance, in my business, I give free marketing advice to anyone that asks, whether they're a customer or not. And, after they purchase, if they want to continue the dialogue, I continue it regardless of whether or not it's likely they'll buy again anytime soon.

To recap, these are the only four reasons people don't buy from you: *No need, no hurry, no money and no trust.*

Increase your sales and profits by responding to these preemptively:

1. Do everything you can to mail your postcards to people and businesses likely to already want your products or services.
2. Make it clear how valuable the benefits of your products and services are to them.
3. Get them to realize the urgency and the value of your products and services NOW.
4. Show them they can trust you by offering security regarding the benefits your products or services offer.

When you do all of these things, guess what? People will buy from you like crazy. Postcards are a perfect, low-cost medium to overcome the four reasons people don't buy from you.

5

CAN'T I JUST USE EMAIL?

This is a question that I hear all the time from business owners, and I understand why — email is cheap, and so are business owners! I know because I am a business owner. We are always trying to find the most cost-effective course of action. While this is a good thing, sometimes we incorrectly evaluate the costs.

Is email cheaper than direct mail? Absolutely, initial expense-wise.

But there is more to evaluate here. I'd like to ask you, the reader, what you prefer. Do you feel trust and affinity for a company — one you've never dealt with before and never given your email address to — if they send you an email to advertise their wares? Do you enjoy being interrupted as you work with emails in your inbox from companies you've never done business with? How do you feel about companies that send you an email that sounds like you've been corresponding with them, but you draw a blank and then realize they're trying to trick you?

The reason people continue to prefer direct mail (as many surveys have revealed over the years) is that they are becoming more and more inundated with junk mail in their digital inbox. I know that I personally HATE getting email from a business that I didn't give my email address to, and I know I'm not alone in that.

So now we need to add to the cost of email the possibility of turning off prospective customers. How much revenue will you LOSE because people got *"spammed"* by you and will now NEVER do business with you? Pretty tough to calculate, I'd say!

Maybe the first 2 times the recipient simply deletes the unwanted email with no emotion whatsoever. But after the third time, you've now totally irritated them. We just don't know. All I can say is, whenever I give a marketing seminar, I ask the audience this question: *"How many of you like receiving emails from businesses you never gave your email address out to?"* I never get a single hand raised in response.

I go on to ask, *"How many of you feel distrust when you get an unsolicited email?"* All the hands go up.

Now the price difference isn't looking so large, is it? Unless, of course, you're not interested in the long-term effects and you just want to make a quick buck and bail. In that case, perhaps it doesn't matter if you upset most of the recipients as long as the instant response is good.

This brings up the classic email marketing debate: Is email a lead generation tool or a follow-up tool?

You will be able to find marketing professionals on either side of the debate, but it will be very heavily against using email for lead generation. I'm hard-pressed to find even one quote in favor of email as a lead-gen tool. However, it was quite easy to get a quote against this practice. Here is one from the website of leading email-marketing provider, iContact:

Having customers sign up directly on your website is a surefire way to build a quality list. Avoid the temptation to rent or buy a list through a third party. Doing this will only cause you problems in the long run. Issues can include poor list quality, increased chance of being flagged as spam and potential loss of reputation.

I invite you to do a Google search on *"email as a lead generation tool"* or something similar. You will get loads of companies eager to sell you a list of email addresses! Please look into this carefully. You will hear *"we don't support spamming,"* *"these are opt-in lists,"* and *"folks gave their email address and want the data."* OH PLEASE! That's all I can say! I'm on those lists and you are, too. Do you really recall GIVING your email address to an opt-in list? Most likely, you forgot to uncheck a box on a fill-in form and BOOM — you opted in!

Yahoo, Gmail, Hotmail and all the larger email service providers do their best to stop companies from abusing their clients' addresses and will block abusers. However, now there are ways to beat the system. My contention is this: if you have to *"beat the system,"* how ethical is that? Okay, I'm ranting a bit now. I need not tell you what side of the argument I'm on. To me, the answer is clear: **email is a *follow-up* marketing tool.**

Yes, some companies in very specific circumstances will have great success generating leads through email marketing. My friend has a company that used to cold call people at home asking if they'd like to change their energy provider. Email is far less intrusive than a call from a stranger during dinner. He has turned to spam to get new clients for this and he doesn't have a problem because truthfully, if he can save them money on their energy bill, they are happy to be informed of this!

However, in most cases, it simply isn't the best way to get leads for your business. It is cheap, but the response rates are dismal (maybe .000005%), and, as we've discussed, there is a VERY good chance you are simply turning off large numbers of potential customers before they ever get a chance to interact with your company.

The optimal use of email marketing is to follow-up with leads you generate through outlets like direct mail, Google ads or television, etc. Once the prospect has agreed to receive communications from your company, they are less likely to dismiss your email or, worse, mark it as SPAM.

By using email and direct mail in the correct way, you maximize your return on investment from your marketing. And that's what we're all after, isn't it?

I'll discuss exactly how to use email as a follow-up tool in Chapter 19: Integrating with Online Marketing.

6

HOW MUCH RETURN
DO YOU NEED?

———————

I have been claiming that postcard marketing is cost-effective, but I haven't really proved it yet, have I? Don't take anybody's word for anything — make them prove it. This chapter is my way of proving it.

When it comes to marketing and promotion, especially in the arena of postcard marketing and promotion, the simplest data is the best. Marketing is not complex if you know the basics.

Many marketing efforts may go unrewarded, not because they were lousy, but simply because they weren't given enough of an opportunity to work. Remembering a product or service is like remembering someone's name; you need to hear it more than once for it to sink in. Showing your TV commercial one time, having a banner ad on the internet one time, or doing one mailing of postcards is almost never enough to grab and keep your audience's attention — let alone get them to buy.

During any campaign, measurement is vital. Without measurement or progress reports, how will you ever know which advertising pieces are the most effective? Be sure to measure your Return on Investment (ROI) in terms of actual MONEY, not by how many people responded.

Wait... that needs to sink in: MONEY, not RESPONSE RATE. Ok, moving on.

It's a lot like dieting. Weight is lost when fewer calories come IN than go OUT. Likewise, profit is gained when more money comes IN than goes OUT. Okay, maybe I'm not telling you anything you don't know, but an advertising vehicle is working when the MONEY it brings in has more value than the MONEY and time spent on the marketing.

Don't become discouraged by a small number of callers responding to a large number of pieces. When it comes to your actual mail piece, *quantity counts*. But when it comes to the response, *quality counts*.

Think about it this way: if you spend several hundred dollars to be in the view of a few thousand possible leads, it may only take a few responses to make enough profit for this type of marketing to be valuable. The usefulness of any vehicle can only be determined after the amount of income generated by the promotion has been calculated. **Response rates are deceiving**; profit is what counts. If you spend one-fifth of what you generate

— or generate five times what you spend — your campaign is a success.

Too often people look at marketing ROI in terms of response rate. In other words, *"I sent out 10,000 pieces of direct mail and only got 39 responses. That is terrible."*

Wrong! You are thinking about response rate, not MONEY.

When it comes to marketing ROI, you have to realize that the *"return"* in return on investment is measured in dollars. Let's say you spend $2,000 to get out a bulk mailing of 5,000 pieces and you get 10 calls as a result. At first glance, it doesn't look like a very good response. But of these 10 calls, you close 6 and get immediate sales of $12,000.

That's marketing ROI! And that's not even taking into account the future sales from those 6 new customers. It also doesn't take into account the people who hang onto the postcard and respond in six months or a year — long after you've made the money from that particular mailing. It could add up to hundreds of thousands of dollars, and all because of an initial outlay of two grand. Just today, a prospect that has been in my database for 5 years spent almost $4,000. My point is, revenue from the initial mailing that captured her attention and then her contact info just paid off 5 years later.

Obviously, you need to keep track of responses from each marketing campaign so you can weed out unsuccessful campaigns and strengthen successful ones. Results of direct mail marketing vary from business to business, but the principle holds and always works: if you send out enough promotion, you will make sales and maximize your marketing ROI. **Don't worry about response rate if your marketing ROI is high.**

It is much easier to sell to a prospect once you get them to call (or come in to your store). As I said in Chapter 2: Two-Step Marketing, step one is getting them interested; step two is having them speak to a representative to get all the details.

So there you have it — postcards are effective and cost-efficient, and I have shown you *why*. With that as our base, we can now move on to crafting the perfect mailing list for your business!

SECTION 2
DEFINING
YOUR MARKET

———

In this section you will learn:

- How to discover who stands to benefit most from your products or services
- How to target your ideal customers with mailing lists
- How to manage your campaign and your mailing lists

7

WHO SHOULD YOU TARGET?

The first step to a successful mailing is defining who exactly the mailing is supposed to reach. There are three main groups you should target with your marketing, and each needs a message specific to them. That is to say, at the very least, you will have three card designs.

In order to have a steady inflow of leads, the three groups you need to target are your customer list, your prospect list and your targeted list.

Group #1: Your Customer List

These are your customers who have already purchased from you, which is why they are so important. If they bought once, they are likely to do it again.

You should repeatedly ask your existing customers to contact you about a specific offer for your products and/or services. A clear, valuable offer with an easy way to contact you is best, and should sound something like this:

25% off your next mailing when you buy 5,000 full-color postcards for $329!

Call 800-628-1804 or visit postcardmania.com/25off.

However, it can be anything you believe they will be interested in based on your personal knowledge of them and, preferably, based on their actual previous buying behavior.

Group #2: Your Prospect List

These are prospects that have inquired about your products and/or services through your own marketing efforts. This group is interested in your service, but hasn't made the decision to *"go for it"* yet. They will be the most likely to respond to a special when you offer it to them.

Group #3: Your Targeted List

The third group is composed of people who should be expected to express interest in your products and/or services, but they have never purchased anything from you or even inquired about your products and/or services.

The likely reason they haven't contacted you is they don't even know you exist — yet. You can remedy that by contacting them with a series of postcards offering a FREE product trial (**Marketing Tip**: always print *"FREE"* in ALL CAPS) or information on the benefits of your products and services. If this list is properly selected — and you make an offer that any reasonable person will find very, very difficult to refuse — then your response rate will be high.

By understanding the needs of these three basic groups, you can craft relevant, effective marketing messages on your postcards to each group. If you market repetitively to each group, you will grow a strong, healthy base of customers and prospects.

8

CUSTOMERS FIRST

Over the years, one thing I've seen over and over again from small business owners is a failure to manage their customers properly from a marketing perspective. I look at customers as an investment, accruing a lifelong balance in the account of relationship-building. Don't create a sale; **create a relationship**.

Customers have given you their ultimate vote of confidence: their money! Now give them a quality product, excellent service and the opportunity to buy from you again and again.

As I said earlier, the first of the three groups you should promote to is your list of existing customers. They are the most likely people to purchase your products and/or services because they have paid for them before. It's not just good for them; it's good for you.

It costs far less money to keep a customer than it does to go out and get a new one. Log that one away. It's like marketing gold. There are three key rules to follow when marketing to existing customers in your company database:

Rule #1: Collect all of their information.

It sounds like a no-brainer, but you would be surprised by how many companies ignore information from their customers. The more information you have about your customers, the more likely you will be able to get in touch with them next time you run a special or want to remind them when it's time to order more products or services.

Make sure you don't neglect to ask for your customers' email addresses. Everybody has one and most will give it up pretty easily as long as you're straight with them. This makes it easy to contact them quickly and efficiently — in a manner they're used to seeing and from a name they trust (yours).

And, if you're already communicating with them via email, don't neglect to ask for their phone number. Once you have their business number, ask for their cell number. If you are in good communication with them, they'll happily give these up. If they don't, you have to work on your ability to get them to trust and like you — but that's a different book by a different author!

Rule #2: Don't treat your customers like prospects.

While form letters and generic emails may be easier for you, don't make the costly mistake of treating your customers like prospects. It is unflattering and bad form on your part. They've spent money with you; treat them appropriately.

To avoid this debacle, make sure you differentiate in your database between people who have placed an order in the past and people who have not. Customers want to feel like you are paying attention to them and when they have placed a few orders with you and are still getting your *"10% Off for First-Time Buyers"* postcards or emails, they tend to feel unappreciated. Remember, if someone doesn't qualify for an offer you are sending out, don't send it to them.

Rule#3: Don't let your promotional designs get too stagnant. When mailing to customers or prospects you have already spoken to, you need to mix things up a bit. Sending the same designs over and over to customers is fine for a while but soon it will cause them to lose interest. Don't misunderstand — I'd rather you send the same design forever rather than stop mailing because you're trying to get around to getting a new design.

Your mailings should be attention-grabbing and informative, not stale and boring. If you recently started offering a new service, a postcard letting your database know about it would be a smart move. The main point is to keep your company in the front of their minds and to keep them reading your postcards.

If you're stuck with an old design, at least you're staying in front of them and THAT is paramount.

Information Sharing = Profit Sharing

Do your customers know that you're open 24 hours?

Are they aware that in addition to selling full lawn care service you can also provide them with the products to do it themselves? Do they know you've opened a second branch closer to them? If so, great. If not, WHY not?

One of your main goals should be to educate your customers about how your product or service works. As a result, they will get more use out of your entire line of products and services. Many times this seemingly complicated process can be achieved as simply as sending out mailings to make your customers aware of ALL you can do for them.

Take, for example, a Minnesota-based home cleaning company called White Glove Cleaning. Not only do they use direct mail postcards to acquire new business, they know how to use them to effectively market to their current customer database as well.

To fully understand how, you will need a little background information. White Glove offers a wide range of cleaning services to homeowners, and in order to maximize the return from their mailings of 5,000 postcards, they send 4,000 to their current customer database and send the other thousand to prospects in the area.

At the beginning of every season, they send out a card advertising their specific services that apply to that season.

For example:
- Winter: Dirty carpets promote germs that cause cold and flu symptoms.
- Autumn: Get carpets cleaned after a busy summer of visitors and dirty kids running through the house.
- Spring: Clean vents, tile and carpets to reduce allergies.

This enables them to serve their customers at the highest level, while also strengthening customer loyalty. Brand loyalty is not something your customers owe you, but something you must earn over time by familiarizing and (re-familiarizing) them with your products and services over and over again.

Sometimes you lose customers because they either forgot who they dealt with last time or because they received some kind of promo from one of your competitors and decided to check it out. It's not your fault; it's simply human nature. Customers want to do what makes their life easier, not yours. If the customer is constantly updated about what is available from YOUR company, they won't spend their valuable time doing research and will be less likely to *"shop around."* This will help to control the normal attrition of your database to your competitors.

White Glove's design for their promotional pieces all have their logo prominently displayed on the front and back — to give each piece the same general feel. Also, picking a company color or group of colors and sticking with it will help to increase recognition and readership of your promo. Simply put, your customers will get to a point where they will read whatever you send them. They need to know it is from your company before they read it. If it doesn't look like what they are used to getting from you, it may go in the trash without a second look.

Being great at what you do is not always enough to keep your hard-earned customers. With all the competition out there today, you need to be constantly reminding your customers **you are the best at what you do**.

Direct mail postcards are the best way to give them that reminder. Always remember to keep mailings that you send to your database informative, attractive and most of all, current.

9

THEN, PROSPECTS

———

The second group you need to market to is what I call your *"Prospects"* list. These are prospects that have actually contacted your business.

Every time someone contacts your business, you absolutely need to get all of his or her contact information. If you make a rule out of this, you will, over time, grow a huge list of prospects that are — or once were — interested in your products or services. This is invaluable to your marketing.

For example, at PostcardMania, 6% of our leads close on the first call. But after a month of keeping in contact, 16% of our leads have closed. After a full year, we're at 25%.

This is the power of marketing to your prospect list.

But if you don't follow up, guess how many you'll close after the first contact?

Zip. Zilch. Zero. Well, actually about 2%.

The practice of continually marketing to your prospect list is called *"follow-up,"* and I will get into more detail on exactly how to do it in Chapter 25. This chapter is about how you can grow your own prospect list, and it starts with a tool I call *"New Caller Sheets."* Not every business owner wants his or her potential customers to *"call in"* and I get that, but keep reading — you'll get the point and be able to apply it in some way to your own business.

New Caller Sheets aka Your CRM (Customer Relationship Management)

When a prospect responds to your marketing and contacts your business, you need to have a system in place that will allow you to capture their identity and contact information. This is important, because as we've learned above, most leads don't close on the first contact.

New lead source information needs to be compiled somewhere so it can be calculated and analyzed. I have found that a great way to do this is with New Caller Sheets.

Here's how it works:

1. First, figure out what data you need from the prospect. This should include at least the following:
   - First and last name
   - Business or home phone number

- Mobile phone number
- Email address
- Their website address (if they're a business)
- How they found out about you
- Any other pertinent data needed by you to help make the sale (industry, product they are most interested in, etc.)

2. Create a New Caller Sheet. This is a sheet of paper or form (or fill-in screen in your database) telling the receptionist or sales rep what data is important to gather and in what sequence.

3. Have the receptionist or sales rep fill in all the data from any new prospect calling (or walking) in. A new sheet should be filled out for each new prospect.

4. At the end of each week, make sure all of the information you've gathered is entered into your Customer Relationship Management software, or at least an Excel spreadsheet. We prefer to have a data entry professional do this rather than having our sales reps do it. The reason for that is when you get into high volumes of leads, you want a great typist entering them so that there are no errors/typos. We lived through this and learned the hard way.

In addition to growing your prospect list, this information can be used to calculate all kinds of things that are useful to know. Take a look and see if there are additional questions you should be asking your leads.

Depending on how leads contact you will dictate whether you can use a New Caller Sheet. You may be able to use a tool to transfer new leads directly into your CRM from the web form they filled out.

Your Website
Another way to grow your house prospect list is to collect your prospects' information through your website. For many businesses, this is the number one way for people to find them. Luckily, it is fairly easy to figure out what pages should have forms on them.

You should have forms on all of your high traffic pages.

In exchange for your prospects' information, you need to offer them something valuable, like a FREE white paper, FREE samples, exclusive content, etc. Filling out a form is nobody's idea of a good time, so you need to make it worth their while.

Once you have instituted these steps, you will begin to grow your very own lucrative prospect list.

For more information on how to market to your prospect list, refer to Chapter 24: Track & Tweak.

10

FINALLY, YOUR TARGETED LIST

The last group of people you should market to are those who have never purchased anything from you before, but can reasonably be expected to be interested. Some companies term this the *"perfect audience"* because these people are those who should be the most interested in your product or service — people that will BUY.

Are you a brand new business? Did you just come up with a great idea for a product or service and dive right in? Or do you already have a going concern — a business you've been working for a while?

Either way, you need to figure out who your perfect audience is. Perhaps it's obvious: You resurface pools, so your audience is homeowners with pools or motels/hotels with pools. Easy.

But if you sell something more generic, like jewelry for instance, where anyone may or may not be your audience, you're going to have to engage in some research to make sure your perfect audience finds you.

Researching Your Own Invoices and History
Sometimes, finding your perfect audience is as easy as researching your own business. For instance, let's say you already have a jewelry store. If this is true, you've already sold lots of jewelry. Who comes into your store and buys? Think about it.

Think about yesterday or last week. Now think less — and look more. In particular, look at the invoices. Take all those invoices and make categories with them: one pile for women over 50, one pile for men over 50. Which pile is bigger? Which adds up to more income? How many invoices were put in neither pile? Maybe most of your clients are under 50. What does that mean for you? How should it affect your promotional efforts?

Also, separate orders by the amount spent. Look at all invoices over a certain amount — say $1,000+. Now go through those invoices and see if the age and gender of the purchaser can be determined. If you keep track of the customer details of who purchases from you, you can figure out who buys most often and spends the most money with very little investigatory work.

Be aware of your misconceptions and fight them with cold, hard facts. Perhaps most of your browsers are women over the age of 50. Do your invoices tell the same story? It could be men between 30 and 50 are doing all the buying. If so, and you've been targeting women over 50, you've been wasting your money. If you can't look over last week's invoices to get an idea of who bought what, start keeping track today, so a month from now you can do a little analysis.

Even if you are not directly involved in selling, don't despair — put your sales staff to work. Have them fill out a form answering certain questions with each sale they make. You'll find most people won't mind answering a few questions. People like talking about themselves, and it will help your sales staff build relationships.

The form can include a little speculation, too. You can have the salesperson fill in what they think the approximate age of the customer is and what that customer's gender is. If the customer uses a credit card, they can ask to see the driver's license and make a note of the date of birth. It's a little sneaky, but doable. It is perfectly acceptable for the salesperson to say, *"We're conducting a brief marketing survey,"* before asking:

- Who are you buying this for?
- Is it for a special occasion?
- What type of piece is it? Ring, bracelet, necklace...
- What do you do for a living?
- What's your zip code?

The more information you have, the better armed you will be later when creating your postcard campaign. Salespeople are usually pretty friendly anyway. They don't have to pull out a form to fill out if it makes them uncomfortable, either. They can just ask casually and fill it in the minute the customer leaves. As long as you get the data and keep a running tally on a spreadsheet — mission accomplished.

This will get you all the important data you need to analyze your customer base. You will discover the truth about who is buying your product so you can target those folks.

NOTE: if all you have is their name and address, there is a fantastic product that will help you pinpoint your ideal customer that you may want to check out. I will discuss it later when we get into mailing lists.

Researching from Scratch

If all this talk of spreadsheets, invoices and receipts leaves you scratching your head and asking, *"What about me?"* don't worry — you're not alone. Let's say you're a jewelry designer and you are opening your very first boutique and you have no idea who will like your jewelry designs.

How will you define your perfect audience? How will you uncover the clues to guide you to the right target market?

Creativity is the answer. Well... creativity and a pair of comfortable shoes. In other words, you are going to have to hit the street — to survey complete strangers (I know!). Go to a busy area with photos of your work or, better yet, bring the actual jewelry with you.

Ask questions and keep very good notes. Which pieces were attractive to which age group? Record that response. What piece stood out the most? Why? Write those answers down.

You also want to know what price point is most acceptable. Come up with lots of valuable questions, and ALWAYS record the response. You don't want to have to do this too often, so the more valuable you can make each *"scouting trip,"* the less of them you'll have to make.

Nowadays you can even use Facebook to perform surveys quite easily. The point is that you need the data to move forward. Any way you can get it will work!

When purchasing a mailing list, the easiest demographics to isolate are age, income, gender and whether or not they are a homeowner. I, personally, would be so bold as to ask some of these questions specifically.

You could say something personal like, *"Hello. I'd like to ask you a few questions. Do you have a minute? Please be honest with me, I'm not seeking any compliments..."*

Then make the best use of the following Q&A:
- Which piece do you like the best?
- Which piece do you like the least?
- What would you pay for that piece? (the one they like the best)
- Do you buy jewelry as a gift for anyone in your life?
- If yes, who?
- May I ask your age?
- Gender?
- Do you own a home or do you rent?
- How far would you drive to shop in a specialty boutique if you really loved what they had to sell?

I know it can be daunting to walk up to complete strangers and ask for their input, but what's the worst that can happen?

Some people won't like your jewelry. Some people will rudely ignore you. Some people won't want to answer all the questions.

BIG DEAL! You need this information to successfully market. Go out there and get the answers so you don't waste your money mailing postcards to a demographic unlikely to purchase. Think of it this way: the more effort you put in now, the less money you'll waste later.

In both examples above — the existing store with receipts to study and the new store canvassing strangers on the street — you'll have to tally up the results of your survey. You are NOT looking for any averages. What you are looking for is the greatest common denominator. If, in the first example above, you find out after 35 sales that 15 of them are to women between 50 and 60, 5 are women over 60, 10 are men between 40 and 50 and the rest are quite varied, what would you do?

I'd ignore the varied responses for now. I'd definitely target women 50+ in age. I would also check the zip codes they live in to see if there are similarities there. Next, I'd add up my 10 invoices from the men and compare them to the 20 invoices from the women. Who spends more? If it's close enough, you may want to target both demographics.

The key here is to do the research now to save time later. Knowledge is not only power, it's profit. The more you know, the smarter you can spend your money on not just your postcards, but the list of who to send them to. As I've shared with you thus far, both are equally important.

I Don't Have a Store

Let's say your particular situation doesn't jive with either example above and you still find yourself with the question, *"Who should I mail to?"*

No worries; I'll give you another example: say you have a product that only goes into American-made cars. And say you notice the customers you have are between the ages of 40 to 60 years old. Well, find out from a list company how many people living in a five or ten-mile radius fit that description. Specifically, 40–60 year olds who own an American-made car. You can absolutely get a list that specific. Or, look at your own customer base and find out where they live. Then find out how many others in their area fit that demographic. That is your list!

Okay, so you get a count of all the records fitting that demographic in the area from a list company and there are 20,000 identities. The catch is you can only afford a fraction of that whole amount to start with. What do you do? Give up because it's too much to do it all at once?

Not a chance. Rome wasn't built in a day; nor will your company be. Simply take 5,000 identities from the 20,000 and start from there. Divide your campaign into three-week segments. Mail out one-third the first week, one-third the next week, and one-third the following week. You can mail the same postcard to all segments of the list.

This strategy makes the best use of your time, money and information. You have successfully targeted a potential perfect audience for your product, identified their numbers and begun a systematic and specific approach to reach them through an initial mailing. Even though it only reaches a fourth of your 20,000 potential prospect list, that's not at all bad for three weeks of work! And you know you have room to grow.

Another audience for your specific product might be distributors of car paraphernalia that sell to auto parts stores. Some of those may want to pick up your product. You'd probably have to sell to them wholesale and there's the chance the product sits on the shelf for a while and you don't get reorders. So, you may want to hit both audiences. You raise awareness with your mailings and maybe the prospect buys at the auto parts store. Or, maybe they order directly from you and you get the retail price. Your list company should be able to tell you how many of these distributors there are nationwide.

Test Mailings

A local HVAC (Heating, Ventilation and Air-Conditioning) business will probably have a pretty easy time getting a solid list of potential clients. Basically, every address in their area has heating and A/C, and that particular universe is most likely small enough to warrant using the whole list. The biggest question for this business will be how much to mail (and that is something we'll get into in Section 4: Campaigning and Tracking).

However, some businesses won't have it that easy. Take, for example, an online retailer of indoor blinds. They have a situation similar to the HVAC business in that almost every house is a potential customer. BUT, every house in the country is far too big a list to hit at once. So this company is going to have to find out which particular groups of homeowners they get the best response from.

There are basically two ways to do this: 1) Pay a research company a lot of money (could be around $10,000 - $20,000) to perform a nationwide survey of potential customers, or 2) Perform test mailings and track the results.

You can probably guess what I'm going to tell you to do.

Test mailings! *Of course.*

Test mailings are a valid form of surveying. There are two major reasons for test mailing surveys rather than interview or online question surveys:

Accuracy
Most of the time surveys are pretty darn accurate, but not always. Test mailings are your actual results, pure and simple. There's no arguing with cold, hard results.

Profitability
If you contract a research company to perform a survey for you, the value you are getting is the information you need to construct your ideal list. If you test mail, the value you are getting back is actual customers responding to your mailings AND the information you need to construct your ideal list.

Both have the same end result, but only one gets you money and customers while you do it. That's a pretty clear decision if you ask me.

◆ In addition to test mailings, you can use your pay-per-click campaign results to help identify your ideal mailing list! These results are similarly accurate and much, much cheaper!

If you are currently doing pay-per-click, log in to your Google Ads account and click on your *"Campaigns."* Then under the keywords tab click on *"Search Terms."* This will show you the exact terms that people are using when they search for your product and service. Incorporate the most popular terms into your postcard design!

Do you want another example? Maybe one more? How about two? Three? I can go on and on, but the important thing to remember from this section is creativity. You have to get a bit clever when figuring these things out.

Aside from postage, your list is typically the most expensive part of the mailing. If you're promoting to consumers it's not too bad, but if you are a B2B (Business to Business) marketer, narrowing down the list to the exact right specifications can get pricey.

Don't worry, though. We'll go over how to evaluate list companies in the next section so you can make an educated decision when buying.

11

ALL ABOUT MAILING LISTS

Your list is an extremely important part of your mailing. It helps you match your product with your customer, one of the most basic factors in successful marketing. Again, I know it still seems complicated, but it's actually fairly simple.

Look at it this way: If you're selling bait, you need to reach fishermen, right? If you're just hitting a zip code or town, only a small portion of the whole will be fishermen, so don't try to reach everyone at once. If you do, most of your mailing will get thrown out or never looked at.

So, how does one go about finding the right list? Once you know exactly who your market is, you can begin researching. In addition to the ways we discussed in the last chapter, there are some companies who specialize in doing most of the work for you.

There are many kinds of lists out there; here's a breakdown so you can decide what works best for you:

Consumer Lists

Google the keywords *"consumer lists"* and you'll get a ton of companies willing to sell you consumer mailing lists. What exactly is a consumer mailing list? A consumer mailing list contains home addresses and/or email addresses of consumers; people who buy products either from brick and mortar retailers or online. These lists are in turn used to sell products and services directly to individuals and families.

Using such a list, you'll be able to break prospects down by age, income, gender, whether they rent or own their home, home value and other variables. Some will include these options (they call them *"selects"*) in their price — others will add on a penny or two per record for this data.

BE CAREFUL. Research well. You want FRESH data. Your consumer list is the most decisive aspect of your direct mail marketing campaign. If you have outdated or inaccurate information, you are wasting time and money following dead-end leads.

Ask these questions to help you choose a list company:

How often is your data updated?

If it isn't 'continuously' — move on.

Do you guarantee deliverability?

The answer should be *"yes."* (Deliverability is the ability of the mail piece to be successfully delivered to the prospect).

What amount of deliverability do you guarantee?

You should agree to no less than 90% deliverability.

Will you refund postage on bad addresses as well as the cost of each bad record?

This is a tough one… 10% is the max on bad addresses as an industry standard. Over the 10%, PostcardMania does refund postage on the bad addresses as well as the cost of the bad address records. I think you'll be hard-pressed to find a list company that will do this, but you might as well ask.

Can I use the list over and over again?

Again, there will be an up-charge for this because quality companies will charge for unlimited use of a list. These compilers are constantly updating their data and there is a cost to that activity. When a random list broker says, *"Sure, use it as much as you want,"* I'm always suspicious. Who compiled that list? In my experience, all the major compilers charge more for unlimited usage.

If it's a *"specialty list"* — meaning everybody on the list has back pain or rides a unicycle or loves painting pottery in their spare time — it's important to ask how the list is compiled. Meaning, how do they know everyone on the list has back pain? Did they buy it from a chiropractor? Be suspicious with specialty lists, ask a lot of questions. Don't just believe it because they proclaim to be an expert.

There are list companies and then there are list compilers. Who compiles this data?

There aren't very many answers to this. InfoUSA is a great compiler. Their data is fresh. They have a great website to get your list counts from, which can be found at www.infousa.com. However, if you're planning on using us for your postcards, you may want us to quote the list for you. Because of the quantity we purchase and because lists are not our main product, we don't need to mark them way up and our pricing usually comes in lower than InfoUSA's retail pricing. Whether you buy the data from them, us or any other list broker, insist the data is fresh and accurate.

You will always get some *"undeliverables"* — this is normal! Businesses and people move all the time.

Don't just buy the cheapest out there, though. Make sure you get the right answers to the above questions. Remember, postage is the most expensive part of any mailing and if the list is old and you get more than 10% undeliverable returns, you are literally throwing money away.

Subscriber Lists

One effective way to target an audience with a shared interest is a subscriber list. Are there magazines your market would be reading? For instance, in our fisherman example, I can think of a half-dozen fishing magazines off the top of my head. In our jewelry example, the choices might not be so obvious, but go to a bookstore and flip through some of the high-end fashion or local magazines. Chances are you'll see dozens of high-quality jewelry ads sprinkled inside.

Magazine publishers will normally rent out their subscriber list. Before you commit, question them on whether they'll allow you to use the list over and over. Often times they have a one-time usage clause in their contract. If so, look elsewhere. Using a list only one time is almost useless.

You need to mail to this list not just once, but over and over again. If they only allow you to mail to it one time and you have to repurchase for additional use, it may get VERY expensive. Then again, if the list is that good, it may be worth it. You'll be the judge of that. It really depends on your ROI (Return on Investment). One of my clients makes $50,000 to $60,000 for every 12,000 postcards they mail out. In that case, repurchasing the list each time is well worth the expense.

Affiliate Companies: Sharing
The key to working with a list-provider is not to reinvent the wheel. I spent years (and a small fortune) learning the ropes from scratch. You don't have to.

Today, more and more companies are willing to offer the lists they've worked so hard to build — for a price. But if you let them do the hard work of trial and error, you can benefit, and the investment you make in that list is a small price to pay. Here are a few examples of this type of list, otherwise known as affiliate companies:

Say you're a mortgage broker. If you're selling mortgages and work with a particular title company, they will sometimes GIVE you their list of clients with address information, loan amount and length of loan. Sometimes, even the lender is included. In turn, they want all your loans closed with them so, in exchange for that, they may share the data they have.

Say you're a florist. You may want to use the recent mailing list of a bridal boutique. Maybe you can provide flowers at a trunk show in exchange for a monthly list of new gown customers. Maybe there is a caterer you sometimes work with that will trade customer lists with you. The point is that you need to get creative. Who may want to use your customer list and also has a good product or service, but doesn't compete with you? Trade with them.

Business-to-Business

When we talk about customers, it's important to define whether you are selling to individuals or businesses. The field of businesses selling to businesses, or B2B, is more popular than ever.

Let's say you are a software-design company specializing in custom databases for a variety of businesses. Well, you're not going to promote to EVERY business. You need to choose the types of businesses that benefit from the type of database you offer.

Maybe you've worked with dental offices or insurance agencies in the past. Well, there are so many different types of both that it can be difficult to prioritize.

Fortunately, there is a way to narrow it down and find the right types of companies to promote to. For example, look for specific business types at https://siccode.com/sic-code-lookup-directory and find out their SIC (Standard Industrial Classification System) codes for these businesses.

B2B: What is an SIC Code?

An SIC code is a four-digit numerical code that stands for Standard Industrial Classification. It is issued to businesses by the U.S. government in order to organize and identify all the different industries in the nation. That way data can be compiled and analyzed about these industries and the government will have uniformity of statistical data collected by the various federal and state agencies and private organizations.

All economic activities are covered, and I quote: *"agriculture, forestry, fishing, hunting and trapping; mining; construction; manufacturing; transportation; communications, electric, gas and sanitary services; wholesale trade; retail trade; finance; insurance and real estate; personal, business, professional, repair, recreation and other services; and public administration."* www.osha.gov/pls/imis/sic_manual.html

B2B: Reading an SIC Code
The first two digits of the code identify the major industry group, the third digit identifies the sub-industry group and the fourth digit identifies the exact industry.

For example:
- 36 = ELECTRONIC & OTHER ELECTRIC EQUIPMENT
- 367 = ELECTRONIC COMPONENTS & ACCESSORIES
- 3672 = PRINTED CIRCUIT BOARDS

If you see a number 9 in the third or fourth digit position of the SIC code, it means it is a miscellaneous industry *"not elsewhere classified"* (NEC). These miscellaneous groups are not made up of similar primary activity groups. They are grouped together and treated as a separate industry.

Why am I telling you all this? Mailing list compilers/companies gather data about a business and one of the ways to sort them is by SIC code. Sure, if you want ALL businesses in a certain gross volume range, then you won't need to know the SIC code.

But perhaps you run a dental lab and you're an expert at a certain kind of bridge. It's obvious you want to promote to dentists. But maybe this particular bridge you specialize in is only used by dental surgeons. There is one code for *"dentists,"* in general, and another for *"dental surgeons,"* in particular. This allows you to get very specific in your search.

Don't leave it to the list company to figure this out for you. They don't know your business the way you do. Compilers NEVER ask questions to determine if the list you're ordering is what you really need to have success with your campaign. You need to understand this material so your list is actually comprised of businesses likely to purchase your product or service, and not just some variance of that industry.

This is vital. Your list will make or break your campaign. The more understanding YOU have about how these lists are compiled and where the data comes from, the more power you will have over the results of your campaign.

Opt-In Lists

This is something you hear people talking about all the time in marketing, but what does it really mean? An *"opt-in list"* is a list that someone puts themselves on voluntarily. They may have signed up for a newsletter within a certain industry and answered *"yes"* to wanting to receive offers or information from affiliates of that company. An affiliate would be any company they sold their list to. It was the business transaction that affiliated them.

Like any list, an opt-in list can be a valuable source of information if used correctly.

The key to all of these lists is that they are just information; you have to make the best out of that information by sending to these lists repeatedly.

Think of how people get on an opt-in list; they checked a box allowing companies to send them information. They're not exactly requesting the information from you, just *"allowing"* it. That's a big difference.

These days, you typically have to uncheck a box rather than check it to not be gathered on such a list. Few people take the time, and thus, end up opting-in. Either way, you have their information; now it's up to you to use it well — and often!

Cloning Your Ideal Customers

What if you could take your very best customers and clone them? You know the ones I'm talking about: they spend the most with you; they keep coming back for more and they tell their friends, family and colleagues about you. Cloning is not going to happen, but there is a next best thing.

It's a service that takes your customer list and analyzes it. It then matches each customer up to one of 70 *"clusters"* that they have separated the entire population into. It gives you all kinds of modeled information about your customers that you cannot find out otherwise. For instance, what magazines they read, how much money they have saved or if they live paycheck to paycheck. Do they have kids? If so, how many? What do they drive? Where do they travel to on vacation? What credit cards do they use? It includes all the obvious things, too: do they own or rent? How old are they? Are they married or single? And many, many more details!

I was skeptical at first and had my former VP of Marketing look himself up. Everything in his *"cluster"* matched him exactly except for one magazine that they said he read — *Popular Mechanic* — and that was the only inaccuracy! He then looked himself up a few years later after getting married and having a baby, and sure enough the new *"cluster"* that they matched him to was spot-on. In a way, pretty scary — big brother for marketing is here. But you can take advantage of that for your business!

Once the analysis is complete, this service matches up similar people to those that already purchase your product or service, and then lets you purchase a mailing list of those people. I call this *"micro-marketing,"* and now you know the secret to successfully cloning your best customers; over and over and over again.

The results are astounding.

Until now, it's been reserved for giant companies with giant marketing budgets. The company that sells this service barely advertises it. Their minimum, bare-bones analysis costs $2,000 and can go up into the tens of thousands of dollars depending on how in-depth of an analysis is done.

It is not my intention to self-promote in this book. Suffice it to say, we have struck a deal with this company that makes it more affordable for small-to-medium-size businesses to use this service.

12

MANAGING YOUR LISTS

If you follow my advice and start mailing to the same list more than once, at some point you will find lists that produce returns (undeliverables) continually. You may notice you start receiving more returns than when you first started mailing to those lists.

You may begin to see things like, *"Undeliverable as Addressed"* or *"Forwarding Order Expired."* Every time you mail to an address and that prospect has moved or cannot be found for any reason, you have just paid for the postage with no possibility of getting a response.

Obviously, it's a pretty big waste of money to continue to mail to these addresses, but what do you do about it? You could simply go into the list of names that you have purchased and delete the returns. No more bad addresses, no more wasted postage, right? That is one option, but there is a better way to handle the situation.

The United States Postal Service has a National Change of Address (NOCA) system that a limited number of companies are licensed to access. These companies are able to take the list that you have purchased, or compiled yourself, and check it against the USPS system. You will receive a report that will let you know if anyone on your list has moved, gone out of business, or even if the zip code that contact was in was changed by the Post Office. Along with the report, you will receive a new copy of your list that has been cleaned and updated.

The cost for having your list checked is very economical (my company charges $50 for up to 10,000 addresses) and will allow you to keep getting your message out to as many people in your list as possible.

At times, you can see up to a 10% undeliverable rate, and it can even be higher on older lists that you have been using for a while. The average is more like 5% undeliverable, so let's take a look at the numbers at that rate:

If you mail 10,000 pieces and get 5% back for bad addresses: 10,000 x .05 = 500 pieces. You will have paid postage on 500 pieces that did not reach their destination. So if you mail to your list again without cleaning it you have just wasted: 500 x $0.35 = $175.00.

If you were to NCOA that list you would have spent $50.00.

So you have three choices when faced with a list that needs cleaning:

1. Spend hours deleting every return that you receive from your list.
2. Waste $175.00 or more in postage and printing every time you mail to that list.
3. Have the list checked by an NCOA service and get back in touch with customers that may have moved, for around 3.5 times less than the cost of mailing again without checking it.

There will also be records that can't be found through NCOA and these you should delete. From our cost comparison, I hope you'll agree that the NCOA service is the easiest and most effective way to keep your postage costs down.

Creating a List with a Newsletter of Your Own

The most effective list you can mail to is one that prospects signed up for. A newsletter (email or print) is an excellent way to build such a list. You probably won't have enough records to make a mailing worthwhile for several months, but start building one now anyway. Before you know it, time flies by and you'll be glad you started, because you'll have a healthy list of prospects and clients who volunteered to hear more about your product or service!

As of this writing, we have about 200,000 subscribers to our weekly *Marketing Like a Maniac Newsletter.* Back when I started collecting, I was inspired by a friend who already had 100,000 subscribers to his newsletter — the company was SunBelt Software. I thought to myself, *"Shoot, it will take me forever to get a decent list!"* But it didn't. Before I knew it, I had 11,000 records! I recall just checking in to see how many we had accumulated and I was shocked and pleased all at once!

In this day and age it is so much easier to do this with the advent of the internet. It's simple for people to find your site, discover your newsletter, type in their email address and forget about it. Every week (or month), you send them a quick, simple newsletter full of facts, tidbits, special offers or breaking news in your industry, and you both win. They get useful information they can choose to read or ignore and you get one more opportunity to offer your product or service.

This is how we did it and how you can do it, too:

Create a monthly newsletter sign-up space on your website. Collect only the email address with the promise that the email address will not be sold and that they can cancel any time.

For the first few months, only send the newsletter to the list — no advertisements at all. But you can definitely have ads in your newsletter and you should.

Ask for feedback in your newsletter. You can offer a submission area where they can vote on how good it looks, the articles it contains, etc. Tweak your newsletter to fit the responses.

When you are getting plenty of kudos for your efforts from your subscribers, then it's safe to send them text and HTML emails. HTML stands for Hyper Text Markup Language. It's the markup language used for creating documents online. Markup language is simply a computer coding system specifying the

layout style of a document. (Definition taken from the Encarta®
World Dictionary, North American Edition.) These are the emails
you get from larger companies with graphics and photos in them.

From these follow up emails, direct prospects to a landing
page on your website which asks for the rest of their contact
information. Give them a good reason to give it to you (free
samples, a free report, a free consultation etc.). If people are
filling in their contact information, you are doing GREAT. This
is a very big deal. You just turned an anonymous email address
into a lead — an actual person that you can now call and mail to.
How often do YOU give strangers a way to reach you by phone or
mail? This tells you that by now your subscribers are comfortable
with you and they are beginning to trust you. You have gained
credibility. Congratulations! This is the very best mailing list for
you to mail to!

SECTION 3
DESIGNING YOUR CARD

In this section you will learn:

- How to design for your target market
- How to design a card that appeals to your audience
- How to craft an offer that pulls results

13

THE MISSING HAT
FOR THE DESIGNER

Which came first: the words or the design? Inquiring marketing minds want to know, but as is the case with so much of marketing, there is no single — let alone simple — answer. Words and design blend together to form what we in the industry call *"impact."* Impact doesn't happen in a vacuum. People respond to words and designs that matter to them. In this chapter, I'm going to put the missing pieces of the puzzle together by talking all about postcard design.

Of course, there's more to creating enticing copy on a direct mail postcard. It's not just the words you use but how you use them — even where you place them and in what order they appear. So if you're not already a graphic designer, I want to get you thinking like one. You need to get into the frame of mind that a designer should have. I'm certainly not expecting you to learn this trade to the point of sitting down at your computer and executing an award-winning design. However, I fully expect you to understand exactly what you need so that you can evaluate any design presented to you by a so-called expert.

Many people think that the quality of any graphic design is determined by how *"pretty"* or visually appealing it is. This couldn't be further from the truth...

Although making the card look good is important, the only true measure of any design, (at least commercially) is, *"How well does it pull?"* By pull we mean what type of response it elicits. Does it pull in calls, pull visitors to your website, pull people into the store or pull people away from the rest of the mail pile?

In essence, does the design accomplish what it set out to do?

That's why we want a *"Response-Based Design"* and not necessarily a *"Gorgeous Design."*

Although both would be ideal. In other words, your designer shouldn't be looking for art awards or best in show; he or she should be looking for a response. I always say that the merit of a graphic designer is based on the performance of his or her designs as opposed to the beauty of them. You may be able to put together the most beautiful ad that the world has ever seen, but if it doesn't make the phone ring it isn't worth the paper it's printed on. If you can create both — something aesthetic that pulls, well then I'd like to hire you!

The following text is a breakdown of the different actions to take and ways to make sure that your beautiful design is also a big-time moneymaker.

BE the Target Market

Every potential customer is different, and they are not naturally inclined to want to listen to advertising. They are going to continue to ignore you, unless you can persuade them to listen. To do that, you have to get into their heads, think like them, BE them.

People respond differently to marketing messages, so you need to know what your target market wants to hear. Then, and only then, will they spend some of their valuable time reading your postcard. The following are a few examples — two products and one service — of how to get the attention of even the most difficult-to-reach prospects on your list:

Example #1 — Product: Wrinkle-Reducing Eye Cream

Who do you need to be in this scenario? Most likely a woman over the age of 40. Try it. Pretend you are a woman over 40 with crow's feet (wrinkles around the eyes, for all you guys) and they are getting worse and worse each day. Did you pretend? Are you her? Good. I'm already her, so it was super easy for me!

Now, how bombarded with advertising is this woman over 40 that you're being? PLENTY! So how are you going to communicate to her in an ad to get her to respond? You may have a headline that pushes the button of how upset she is about those crow's feet like, *"Crow's Feet Getting Worse as You Age?"* You may want to show a before-and-after image. Now you've got her attention — and you're halfway there.

Example #2 — Product: A New Golf Ball (that goes farther and straighter than the competition)

Middle-aged women aren't the only ones getting blitzed with heavy-duty marketing these days. Golfers are another saturated market, so in the case of pitching a new golf ball you'd want to create different messages to target different markets.

So, let's pick one to demonstrate with: Your target market is senior citizen golf enthusiasts in the state of Florida. First, I want you to figure out what the number one benefit of this particular product is for that target market. To answer that question, you should use three things:

Reasoning:

You have to think about certain attributes of senior citizens.

Experience:

Do you know any seniors that enjoy golfing?

Research:

If you do, then call a few up and find out what they have to say about their golf game as they got older.

In this case, in particular, I can tell you from stories I've heard that the older the guy is, the straighter the ball goes. Practice makes perfect and older people have generally had much more practice. Also, as people get older they start to lose strength overall. This means that they will start to lose distance on their shot. It is relatively easy to tell that the distance factor is going to be the biggest benefit for them — and therefore should be the focus of the ad.

Also, this audience, in particular, will want a direct design. How about a putting tee with the words *"You Are Here!"* pointing at your ball sliding into the cup? Again, we're not calling for Picasso here; just a response- based design that is sure to get your prospect's attention!

Example #3 — Service: Home Refinancing

You're designing a card for a mortgage broker in this case. This example has you trying to determine the biggest benefit of refinancing a mortgage for families with a household income of $75,000, revolving debt of $15,000 and over two children. Sound complicated? It can be.

The question to ask yourself is, *"What visual would appeal to this market?"* Would it be a fixer-upper theme for home repairs? Luggage and passports to appeal to their wanderlust for travel? A boat or some other luxury?

Maybe the benefit is getting cash to pay off their debt; maybe it's paying for college or even lowering their monthly payments. There is no real way to tell just by looking at the situation. Now you are going to have to do some research.

Research the Target Market for What to Say: Two Essential Questions for Prospects

Research can be as in-depth as actually phoning some of the people in the target market and conducting surveys or as simple as looking at your experiences with past customers. If you decide to survey, here are some good questions to ask:

Question 1: What do your top five customers' orders have in common?

Do they all purchase a certain add-on? Is there a service that none of them take advantage of? This will help tell you what a *"good customer"* actually is. (We'll get back to this mortgage refinancing example in a few paragraphs.)

Question 2: What is the most-often-stated benefit of your service?

In order to learn more about your industry (or if you are a designer — your client's industry) you must ask: Is it something specific about the product? Is it service? Is it price? Ask your customers. They know and you need to know for obvious reasons. This is one where you can BE the customer to a degree, but from my personal experience there is nothing better than asking. If you were to ask 20 customers, *"What, precisely, is the greatest benefit Company X's service or product has provided you?"* 10 may have the same answer while the other 10 have varied answers.

For instance, let's say you sell and install window treatments. You find out from reviewing your invoices that a certain blind sells exceptionally well and most of the customers that purchased them live on the water or in a high-end part of town. (It just so happens it's a fairly expensive product.)

You know that this particular blind never fades and helps keep heat out of the room. You may assume that this product sells to a high-income homeowner because of these incredible features. But upon surveying that demographic, you find they simply chose what they thought went with their décor and felt would add style to their home.

If you were to advertise this product with the features YOU thought were so valuable, you may or may not be pulling in the recipient's attention with that headline. They may or may not need that problem solved. You may find the majority of people say your sales rep Tom is so handsome and charming that most housewives buy whatever he recommends and he has a bent for this particular blind.

You honestly may not know how your customers respond until you ask.
I mean, if all your customers shout out in delight about the very same feature or benefit of your product, by all means, go with what works. I am in no way suggesting you reinvent the wheel when it comes to designing your postcard, but merely look at the design not just from your standpoint, but the standpoint of your customers.

Heck, maybe you should put Sales Rep Tom's handsome mug on that baby! It may not be your idea of an aesthetically-pleasing postcard, but remember, that's not the true test of a good postcard design — what *pulls* is!

Now let's revisit that targeted family we are trying to help refinance their home: Pretend you are a family man or woman with a household income of $75,000 with revolving debt of $15,000 and you've got two kids. Kids can be pretty expensive. So, why would you like to refinance?

I'm not going to give you the answer this time. It's up to you to *"BE"* the recipient and then engage in some research and use your own good reasoning to figure it out. I know you can come up with it because we have a host of young designers here at

PostcardMania that don't have kids yet or a mortgage and they've figured it out! All it takes is a vital imagination and the ability to role play; two qualities most small business owners have in droves!

What do you want the customer to do?
(If you don't know, how can they?)

Since you have now figured out what the customer needs to read and see to be interested, next you need to figure out what it is you want from them. What are you trying to accomplish? Sometimes it is as simple as getting them to go to your website for more information. Other times you are looking for them to pick up the phone and actually place an order. Either way, spell it out for them.

We're not writing a mystery novel here; whatever it is that you want your customer to do, you need to state it clearly on the postcard.

Don't mince words and whatever you do NEVER sacrifice clarity for cleverness.

I repeat: don't sacrifice clarity for cleverness.

For example, if you want them to call and talk to a representative, the card should very clearly say, *"Call today and speak to one of our representatives for more details."* This simple statement tells the customer exactly what you want them to do.

It even tells them when to call: today.

Remember, response-based design is addressing their response, not yours.

Writing cryptic messages or riddles, using artsy references or literary quotes, copying famous artists' poses or hiding mouse ears in your designs may make you and your close, intimate circle of friends smile, but if your customers don't get it, what response are they likely to give?

That's right — none.

Believe it or not, people like to be told exactly what to do in advertising. They appreciate fun, whimsy and cleverness, but not at the cost of clarity. You should make it as easy as possible to make the requested action. The more your prospects have to think, the less likely they are to actually act.

Case in point: how many clever commercials have you seen on TV that you have no idea WHO the company was or WHAT the product is — let alone what they want you to DO? Personally, I LOVE the stop-motion video Kindle commercial — it's beautiful! Great song and fun to watch! But, how many times did I have to see it to figure out what the heck they were promoting. AND THEN every time it came on I'd think to myself *"what are they promoting again?"* until the end... when I'd see the word Kindle. I just wonder how much money they spent on airtime for all those ads?

Another key part of the call to action is supplying the proper supporting information along with the request. In this case, the phone number should be prominent and be the closest element to your call to action. Common sense would seem to say as long as the phone number is somewhere on the promo, they will find it and give you a call. However, the reality is that if the number isn't right there for them to see, your response rate will drop considerably.

Make sure the call to action is bold and easy to understand. Keep any important contact information in close proximity to the call to action. Remember, postcard design should err on the side of being less artistic and more simplistic.

What should it look like?

The *"look"* of a direct mail postcard is a subject of much debate, so I am only going to give you my experience from over a hundred thousand clients and over half a million postcard campaigns. I've seen the flops and I've seen the raving successes so, if you only trust me on one issue, trust me on this one.

Let's start by evaluating one of our clients.

The owners of Measurable Solutions, a business management consulting company, know how to market. So much so that they made none other than Entrepreneur Magazine's *"Hot 100 List"* — this is a list of the fastest-growing new companies in the country.

Clearly, these guys know how to get the phone to ring and the truly amazing part about their postcard campaign is that for the first four years of their business they only promoted to one mailing list of 30,000 names.

They started by providing their service to one industry — physical therapists who own their own practice.

I love this story because we didn't design their card and I

learned something really fascinating from them. You see, I am a graphic designer. So my background dictates that the card has to be aesthetically pleasing to the recipient. These guys proved me so wrong!

Not only did they completely wring out of my brain that idea, but they also taught me something else: sometimes to BE the customer you have to actually BETRAY what you think about that customer.

What Measurable Solutions does, in a nutshell, is business management consulting. I know, sounds pretty hoity-toity, high brow, conservative, intelligent... right? And who they do it for is doctors who own their own practice, specifically physical therapists that own their own practice.

So you may automatically assume that you need a conservative-looking postcard, especially if you're mailing to doctors that have never heard of you. Right?

This really drove home *"BE"* the recipient to me. Think about it. A doctor with his own practice is a man or a woman — just a person really, right? A woman or a man with a personality, likes, dislikes, problems and the rest. What is going to communicate to this person?

Well, Jeff Lee and Shaun Kirk, the owners of Measurable Solutions, surveyed them to find out. They didn't assume anything and this is the art they presented to us to use on their business launch postcard:

I cringed inside, smiled politely and said, *"Are you sure this is what you want to use?"*

LIE #27, as told to PTs in Private Practice:

The only way to
Get New Patients
is to go out and
MEET and FEED DOCTORS.

(For the **TRUTH**, see the other side...)

" ' I know everyone does it, but that doesn't make it right.' Ever hear that when you were a kid? Well, here we go again. In most practices, when the numbers are down, 'someone' has to go out and talk to doctors. In a small practice it's usually, 'Tag, you're it!'

Have you ever had times when you met with a doctor and felt he or she was interested in what you had to say, but you still walked away empty handed? Well, the reason that happens is because it's bad manners not to seem polite. Tell me you've never done this with a vendor coming in to sell you something. You're polite and appear interested, but you know you're not going to buy. Well, doctors do the same thing ..."

Shaun Kirk, MHS, PT, MTC
Pres., Measurable Solutions

MEASURABLE SOLUTIONS, INC.
420 S. Garden Avenue
Clearwater, FL 33756
Phone: 1-800-491-2828
www.measurable-solutions.com

PT6

LEARN THE TRUTH:
HOW TO HAVE NEW PATIENTS
OUT THE WAZOO!!

Ask for our FREE CD. Call 1-800-491-2828
or go to: www.measurable-solutions.com

Postcard Design Provided by Measurable Solutions, Inc.

Well, they mailed this card over and over to the same 30,000 doctors for years.

The color pops, I imagine it makes them smile, and it solves the most common problem discovered from surveying — not enough patients.

After more surveying, they found another problem these particular doctors deal with: to be able to treat a new patient, that patient has to be referred by an MD. Shaun and Jeff found out physical therapists (PTs) all over the country lure these MD's to refer patients by FEEDING them. Yes — buying them meals. They also discovered PT's absolutely loathe this activity. They simply consider it a necessary evil.

So despite its obvious lack of artistic merit, its design imperative is impeccable; this postcard answers those points in a way PT's find comforting and the folks at Measurable Solutions find profitable. In the end, that's the true test of an effective design.

The point I'm trying to make is this: The beauty of the design is secondary to the message; and it's secondary to whether or not the message communicates directly to the recipient.

To this day, Measurable Solutions has never changed their successful action of a simple, bright yellow card with legible and immediate communication. They've never tried to add an *"aesthetic"* image to what has already been working so well. Would an aesthetic image pull even better results for them?

Maybe — maybe not.

Regardless, they're not willing to take the risk, and I don't blame them. If it were up to me, I would probably do a test mailing with a great image to a small portion of the same list and compare. On the other hand, *"If it ain't broke, don't fix it."*

14

12 ELEMENTS OF A SUCCESSFUL DESIGN

A picture may be worth a thousand words, but an effective postcard design is worth a thousand prospects.

The design of your postcard is almost as important in eliciting a response as getting a good list — it runs a very close second. Much as in deciding on a list, there are definite rules you should follow when designing a postcard.

Based on what I said earlier about the quantity of mail determining your income, you could literally slap together a postcard on your own printer, send it out consistently, and still make money. However, there is more to direct mail marketing than the bare minimum, and eventually low quality will start to affect your campaign. Since you are reading this book, I take it that you want to know how you can utilize direct mail to really grow your company. And that requires far from the bare minimum.

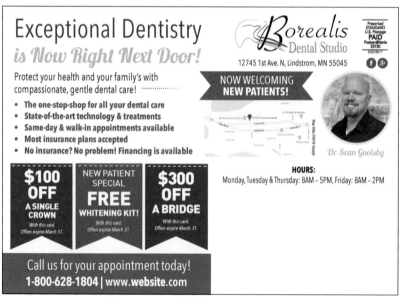

Postcard Design Utilizing the 13 Elements

Do you want your direct mail postcard to end up in the trash with the rest of the unread mail?

These are the 12 (or 13 for some businesses) elements your design absolutely must have to maximize your return:

1. **A clear, bold headline**

   On the postcard there should be one central message. The best way to achieve that is with a bold, clear headline that isn't cluttered up with other text. The headline should allow the recipient to immediately know what you're selling. The key word being *"immediately."*

2. **A graphic that supports the message**

   The graphic should be easy to understand and add to the message the headline is conveying. For instance, if you are trying to get people to list their home, you would want to show a home with a SOLD sign clearly visible out front. That graphic reinforces the message more than a plain picture of a home.

3. **Color that pops**

   Make the headline and other text stick out by using a color that stands out from the background color. When you look at the card, ask yourself, *"What do I see first?"* If it isn't the headline, you might want to tweak the colors or increase the size of the headline.

4. **A subhead that leads into text**

   If you have a couple paragraphs of text with no lead in on the back of your postcard, there's nothing to entice people to read the copy. A subhead will give prospects a place to start reading. If you have only a hundred words or so, you may be able to get away with it, but if the text gets any longer the average reader will need some guideposts along the way.

5. **Benefits, benefits, benefits**

   One of the biggest errors people make in advertising is stating features, rather than benefits. For example, never assume recipients know what benefit can be derived from a lower interest rate on their mortgage. Instead, let them know their monthly payments will go down.

6. **The offer**

   An offer is always a good idea and should represent a specific reason to call NOW, such as *"Limited supply"* or *"Interest rates are climbing,"* or *"Save $50 before the end of the month."*

7. **Your company name and logo**

   Although this needs to be on the mailer, it shouldn't overshadow the offer. Customers care most about what you can do for them — not who you are or how great you say you are.

8. **Call to action**

   Tell prospects exactly what you want them to do. *"Call today for more information"* or *"See us online"* are two of the most common desired actions. What happens when they see you online could be the subject for another book — this is very important. Another great way to get people to see your offer and call to action is to position them near each other and in a color that doesn't match the rest of the design. That way, their eye will be involuntarily dragged to your offer and call to action (CTA).

9. **Contact information**

Provide your phone number and web address directly following the call to action. Whatever you ask prospects to do, give them the means to do it — right away. Don't make them search for it.

10. **Return address**

A return address ensures you'll get returned mail from the post office and communicates you're an established professional. People feel better knowing the company they're dealing with has an actual location.

11. **A 5-star review**

Don't give the recipient the added step of searching for reviews online. Provide one on your card. Even if you are brand new, you can get someone you serviced to say something great about you and put 5 stars next to that quote. If you have a huge number of 5-star reviews online, brag about it on your card!

12. **QR code**

A QR code (short for Quick Response) makes it easy for people to jump right from your postcard to your website with minimal effort. They only have to scan the QR code with their smartphone camera, and a link to your website or landing page pops right up. QR codes can also be used in your CTA with verbiage like, *"Scan me!"* Just make sure that the web page you're driving your postcard traffic to is set up for success — meaning it has a form people can fill out to redeem an offer with a high perceived value, thereby capturing that lead for you.

13. **CONDITIONAL — A map of your location.**

Are you a local or regional business that people visit with or without an appointment? Add a map to the back of the card with the little red upside-down teardrop and the nearest major roads so people know where you are at a glance.

* Also — make sure you don't use specialized terminology that only other professionals in your industry will understand. I've seen this mistake A LOT. If a recipient reads something that is completely foreign to them, they WILL NOT ACT.

The Ultimate Postcard Success Test

Answer the following questions honestly, and then tally your score. Anything less than a perfect 13 means your postcard (and investment) is at risk!

1. Does your postcard have a crystal clear headline?
2. Is there an eye-catching graphic that supports the message of the headline?
3. Does the color scheme make the postcard *"pop?"*
4. Is there a sub-headline on the back of the postcard that continues the message from the front of the card?
5. Does the copy focus on the benefits of your offer (rather than the features)?
6. Is there a compelling offer (special benefit, discount, etc.) to spur the recipient to action?
7. Is your company name and logo featured on the postcard?

8. Is there a call to action that spells out exactly what the recipient needs to do to respond and is the eye dragged there involuntarily?
9. Is there a 5-star review that includes a 4-star graphic?
10. Is your contact information on the postcard?
11. If (and only if) you're local and support foot traffic, did you include a map with your location highlighted and your largest crossroads clearly outlined?
12. Does your design include a QR code linking to a web page that's set up to capture the identity of recipients?
13. Is there a return address (ideally not a P.O. Box) on the postcard?

Understanding Your Score

0-6

Eek! You are missing CRUCIAL elements in your postcard. It is unlikely you will have success with the postcard as-is.

7-9

You have a chance. You have enough elements to give you a shot at success, but your best bet is to tweak your design so that all 13 of the elements are included.

10-13

Nailed it! You are good to go. Mail those puppies and watch the prospects roll in.

15

BENEFITS, BENEFITS, BENEFITS.

Words are more than just letters strung together to convey meaning; words are powerful, living, vital things that create responses in your listener or reader. Since what you say, who you say it to and how you say it are key parts of designing effective direct mail pieces, you need to know the words that sell.

Naturally, I'm going to share them with you here...

Let's Look At What To Say:

It is vital you get attention fast. If you don't, your offer will not be read. Here's how to do it:

Brag about the benefits: An excellent way to get attention — and hence get read — is to boldly give the 5 or 6 key benefits of your product or service. Put the biggest benefit on top and list off the rest in descending order of importance. For example:

How would you like to get...
- Biggest benefit (such as *"lower monthly payments"*)
- Second biggest benefit (such as *"higher equity"*)
- Third biggest benefit (such as *"more resale value"*)

You get the idea.

Make your benefits appealing: People are interested in things they want. If your benefits are really beneficial to them, they will read your postcard. (If your list is good and you really know what benefits your ideal customer is seeking, they will respond too.)

Be specific: The next thing to do is give a very brief explanation of how you can provide the benefits you named.

Contact is key: Next, persuade them to act by giving them a good reason to contact you. Trust is a key factor here, so begin building yours immediately. For instance, you can have a 5-star review from a really happy customer right on the card.

Delete risk: If you have or can give a guarantee, give one. Guarantees take the risk away for the person receiving your postcard.

Make it easy to agree. Make them an offer that no reasonable person who had an interest in your product or service could easily refuse. Make sure it has a very high perceived value but doesn't cost you very much at all.

How should you say it? Probably with the fewest amount of words as possible. Picture the size of a typical postcard; they're bigger than a business card but not quite a flyer. That's the amount of room you're working with. So words are at a premium and not to be wasted. I recommend using bullet points over paragraphs of text. You are not trying to close them on the card. You are simply trying to move them through the buying process, hopefully to take the next logical action — either call, show up or go to your website.

For example: *"Now is your chance to take advantage of our special offer. Don't miss out. Call NOW!"* Then follow up with these two top tips:

Make it simple: Be sure to explain exactly how to order or contact you for further information.

Guarantee: When you include a guarantee on your postcard, you are almost guaranteed to get a good response — no pun intended.

16

TWO TYPES OF POSTCARDS: STATIC & VARIABLE

———————

Just when you're thinking you've got a handle on this whole *"postcard marketing"* thing, I'm going to kick a little sand on your fire: there are actually two kinds of postcards that you need to know about!

Cue threatening theme music.

But fear not! The distinction (while important) is actually quite simple, and I'll explain it now.

There are two types of postcards: Static and Variable.

Static postcards are the most common and traditional type of postcard. This is when a design is created, and the exact same design is mailed to everyone on the mailing list. So, everyone would get a card that looks like this:

Static Postcard

Variable postcards have designs that can actually change based on who the recipient is. The easiest example is a postcard personalized with the recipient's name. Everyone gets a similar looking card, but each postcard is customized with the specific name of the person receiving it. This type of postcard requires relatively recent technology, and while they are not as common as static postcards, they are becoming more and more popular with each passing day, for reasons that will be clear to you in a moment.

But before I get to those reasons, here's a quick note on that technology I mentioned: it's actually been around for longer than you'd think. However, until recently, it was so expensive to use that barely anyone did. Once the technology (known as Variable Data Printing) became affordable for small businesses, variable postcards began to really take off.

Essentially, Variable Data Printing (VDP) is a computer program that pulls data from your mailing list and then adjusts the postcard's design to reflect that data. So instead of everyone getting the design above, you can tell the program to customize the card with the recipient's name, and you'd get designs like this:

Variable Data Postcards with Variable First Name

And then you can get more specific and tell the program to use a masculine or feminine image, based on the recipient's gender, like so:

Variable Data Postcards with First Name & Gender Variables

And even more specific by testing out different offers based on the specific neighborhood the recipient lives in:

Variable Data Postcards with First Name, Gender & Offer Variables

As you can see, the level of personalization adds up quickly. And THAT is the reason more and more businesses are switching to variable postcards. Think about it...

When you're in a busy, crowded place, and you hear someone shout out your name, what do you do? Consciously ignore it and keep going? Or do you automatically turn to see if it's for you?

I do the latter, and I bet you do too. Now, let's go to a whole-notha-level. Let's say we're talking about a prospect, and the busy, crowded place is their mailbox... See where I'm going with this?

If your postcard shouts their name AND is tailored to their specific interests, concerns, etc., they are way more likely to stop and give their attention to it. And with variable postcards, now there is a way to do just that!

NOTE: Most printing companies have their own term for Variable Data Printing. Some call it that. Others use terms like "custom postcards" or "digital printing." At PostcardMania, we call our product Personalized Postcards. It's all pretty much the same thing. Just wanted to clear that up for you!

17

THE OFFER

It may seem counterintuitive to give your customers a price break when you are struggling with your revenue, and it may seem crazier to give them one when they are lining up to pay your normal rates, but there is more to it than meets the eye. Allow me to explain...

There are two major functions that an offer (special rate, sale, discount, etc.) plays in your marketing campaign:
- Enticing new customers to try your product or service
- Rewarding current customers and ensuring future loyalty

In a successful marketing plan, these are your two main goals. Neglect new prospects and your business will plateau. Ignore your current customers and your business will see high customer turnover, and plateau — right before it drops off a cliff!

Here are some tips you can use to reinforce your marketing:

Marketing to New Prospects

The offer you present to prospects will be different from what you offer to your customers. It needs to have the following attributes:

High Value

Do your homework. Come up with something that would be considered a great value in your industry.

Good example: FREE iPad with Braces!

It is of high value to the prospect, and it gives you the chance to WOW them with your service and professionalism.

Bad example: 10% OFF Haircut & Style

The incentive is not valuable enough to inspire action. Nobody jumps at 10% off.

Low Cost

The prospect needs to feel as if they are getting a steal, especially if they're trying something for the first time. Don't be afraid to offer a product or service for free. The profit you gain from a lifelong customer far outweighs the price of a free promotion.

Good example: FREE!

Anything FREE is enticing. But don't attach many strings or you will lose the customers' trust.

Bad example: $400 OFF Landscaping Package!

You may know that's a great savings, but if the dollar amount is too high, it may frighten away your prospects.

Believability

Good example: Buy one sweater, get a second one free!

It is believable. The customer understands the cost involved and will think it is a great value.

Bad example: FREE* Phone!

The customer instinctively (thanks to that asterisk) knows you're not giving them a phone for nothing and will not trust you.

Our results manger tracks successful offers based on the industry. Here are a few examples that were great successes for my clients:

- Dental — FREE Teeth Whitening for Life
- Chiropractic — FREE Massage with X-rays if necessary ($260 value)
- Landscaping — First Two Lawn Cuts FREE
- Restaurant — Celebrate your anniversary with a FREE dinner on us!

These were successful for our clients because they offered something that had a high perceived value — for free! Free is great because it has automatic value for consumers. But as long as your prospect feels they are getting a great value, it will work.

Remember: price differs in many industries. A free massage and X-rays at Benson Chiropractic is worth $260, while a free dinner at The Grotto restaurant may be worth $15, but both were successful deals because the offer was valuable within their respective industries.

Offers to Current Customers

To tailor an offer to your customers, you need to follow the same basic principles as a new prospect offer, but with an added condition.

The Offer Must Have:
- High value
- Low cost
- Believability AND
- A reward

Your customers need to know they are getting this deal as an exclusive reward for their loyalty and because you value their business. This is not an attempt to draw them in — you've already done that!

Here are some examples of what reward offers look like:
- Dental — FREE cleaning on the anniversary of your first visit!
- Jewelry — A *"secret sale"* scratch-off coupon to customers who spent over $100 in a month!
- Skin Care — $30 off next purchase and a FREE sample product!
- Theater or Entertainment Services — Save $10 off your next ticket!

Whatever your offer may be, let me stress that the offer is incredibly important and can — along with other things — make or break your results. I also feel I must impart that this has been my personal nemesis at my own company. Honestly, I have yet to find the end-all offer to bring in hordes of qualified leads. Don't get me wrong; we're doing great and pretty much have our marketing down to a science, but that end-all enticing offer is still eluding me!

However, I have seen some incredible offers that pull brilliantly for the marketer.

One comes to mind in particular. This client is a credit union. I don't think they thought of what they did as *"an offer"* separate from any other aspect of their card, but they gave such an incredible rate on a CD that had I, myself, received their postcard I would have transferred my savings over too!

After reviewing their results and their ROI (Return On Investment), it became very clear to me just how important the *"offer"* actually is. I'll share an email one of my sales reps received:

Rob, just received one of your marketing pieces in my email, and noticed this line from it: 'A one-shot-in-the-dark postcard mailing is not going to change your business, your bottom line, your life or your anything.'

As a long-time professional marketer, I would generally agree with that. However, I just thought I would share the results of the last postcard job you did for us. You may or may not recall doing the blue castle-in-the-clouds postcard for Texoma Community Credit Union back in April-May. It advertised some great CD rates, and said, 'Your big dreams deserve a big rate.'

You printed 5,000 for us, 2,400 of which you mailed for us to a list of homeowner-investors that we purchased from Database USA. We mailed an additional 1,000 to our top depositors, and handed the rest out in our two credit union lobbies. We were extremely pleased with the quality of the paper and printing you did for us.

Our initial goal was to raise $1 million in CD deposits in May. During the month of May, the postcard brought in $5.3 million in CD deposits, surpassing our goal by well over 400%. Needless to say, we were quite pleased!

Our ROI calculations came out quite nice: We spent $610 on printing and $670 on postage, for a total of $1,280.

We generated 198 CDs, totaling $5.31 million, with the average CD balance of $26,816. We use the "spread" between the interest we earn (on auto loans, for example) and the interest we pay out on CDs to calculate our ROI. In this case, the business your postcard brought in generates $9,336 per month in net income to the credit union, which gave us a break-even point of just 4 days, and a 12-month ROI of 8,652%.

Not bad for a one-time postcard mail-out! By the way, I have entered this postcard (and the latest brochure you printed for us) in this year's Texas Credit Union League marketing competition. I'll let you know (in October) if we win!

Just thought you might want to hear a success story. Feel free to share this as appropriate.

Sincerely,
Mike Segalof
Marketing Director
Texoma Community Credit Union

Needless to say, when this was forwarded to me I knew I had to include it in this manual. We called him immediately to verify the data — I mean, 8,652% ROI may have been a typo! But it wasn't. Mike came up with a great design and headline that caused the recipients to READ the card. If he hadn't, that offer would not have been looked at and the card would have most likely wound up in the trash. So, you see, all the variables in designing your postcard are important.

Loss Leader as an Offer

During the holidays we often hear how much more important it is to give than to receive. In business, sometimes it's important to give so you can receive.

That's where a loss leader comes in.

A loss leader is when a company or store sells one product at a loss in order to bring customers into the store KNOWING they'll spend on other items where they can make a profit. For example, Office Depot will advertise reams of copy paper for $1.99 per ream. But when the small business owner arrives to purchase it, he/she remembers to buy pens, calculators and oh yeah, a new laptop.

This is a great idea and generates big results for the big dogs in retail. But how can it work for you? See if there is any way you can incorporate this into your postcard offer. Maybe there is a product that's not moving very well. If you offer to discount it, you not only bring customers to your storefront or website, but you also draw them in to make bigger purchases as well.

Seriously, give it some thought. See what you can come up

with. Survey your customers to see if it would make them come in and don't forget to put this very important ingredient into the mix when designing your postcard.

The Two Rules of Using Offers to Improve Your Response
Rule #1 — REWARD those who buy now.
Rule #2 — PENALIZE those who don't.

How? Satisfy these two rules with a *"very special offer"* that a) is attractive and b) has a time element attached to it. Try something like this: *"Order your new lawn mower NOW and we'll give you a FREE edger. Offer only good until the end of May."*

This offer is attractive because you get a free edger; it has a time element because there's a strict cut-off date: the last day of May. Furthermore, those who buy now are rewarded with a free edger (Rule #1). Those who don't buy now miss out (Rule #2).

Warning: Obviously, the offer must be financially feasible for you, so you'll have to do some number crunching before you make the offer. But if you can't make the numbers crunch, get creative. People love FREE stuff (there are those ALL CAPS again), and often don't read the words that follow F-R-E-E that closely. If you can't make the FREE edger from our above offer work, offer a coupon for a FREE cleaning or a FREE booklet on how to keep the lawnmower clean. Neither are very expensive, and both continue to make the offer attractive.

People expect more these days. Think about it: Google is FREE, Facebook is FREE, WiFi is often FREE. In order to have an attractive offer, the prospect has to really feel they're getting a deal. FREE is a great way to do that.

You can tie these special offers in to some particular event or season (like jewelry or flowers or chocolates for Valentine's Day or just about anything for Christmas), but you don't have to.

Special offers help you maximize your direct mail marketing efforts and keep your customers ordering from you when you want them to. It's just one more way to be in control of your promotion.

The customer may always be right, but he's not always in charge.

YOU can control how much — and how fast — your company grows.

18

THERE ARE WEBSITES & THERE ARE *WEBSITES*

I told you I could write a whole book about this, but here I have to at the very least give you a chapter. Your postcard marketing results have a lot to do with your website. Ninety five percent (95%) of the people that are interested in what you're promoting will go to your website first — before taking any other action. (Well, they might read reviews first but that's for another chapter entirely.) What occurs for them at that visit will affect whether or not they do business with you.

Think about it: what happens when you visit a website? Don't you immediately begin to form opinions on that company, either subconsciously or consciously? Of course you do. We all do. That's why it is so important that your website builds trust and raises affinity with your prospects and visitors right away.

If your site is too slow, hard to navigate or difficult to understand, you won't gain trust or build a rapport with the visitor and, as a result, lose business. You don't want that.

You see, it is no longer a luxury for you to have a website, it is a necessity. Consumers expect one. But not only a website — an EFFECTIVE website.

Here are ten ways to go from *"having"* a website to having an EFFECTIVE website (this minor education should help reduce the pain most people experienced in the development phase of their site as well!):

1. **Clean up your homepage.**
   Cluttered homepages have visitors running for the *"back"* button faster than you can say *"there goes that lead."* Your homepage should clearly and simply present who your company is, what you provide/offer, how to contact you and a reason to visit your other pages for more information.

2. **Don't over-design — it's not an art contest.**
   It doesn't matter how impressive your fancy Flash introduction is if nobody knows what you can do for them. People use the internet to get information. Unless you are a graphic designer displaying your portfolio, keep the crazy Flash over-designing to a minimum. Make sure every graphic supports your message. If it doesn't — ditch it.

3. **Make it easy to navigate.**
   If your *"About Us," "Products/Services"* or other pages are not clearly placed, people won't bother finding them. As a general rule, go by the two-click rule. Prospects should be able to get

to any page on your site in two clicks. This is ideal. If it takes more than four, nobody will bother.

4. **Keep your URLs (website addresses) and links short and sweet.**

   Choose simple, informative URLs for your site. You want your URLs to be easy to remember and contain keywords that are easily identified by search engines. Just to be clear — people type keywords into Google searching for what you have. If you can incorporate one or more of those words into your website address, you will be found faster than if you don't. For instance: my husband's company is called Blue Streak Docs. Even if you go to bluestreakdocs.com, you will see the address instantly changes to bluestreakdocumentretrieval. com. Document Retrieval is what folks would search for when they need his service, so he has that URL.

5. **Focus on your content.**

   The words on your site sell your company. Always list the BENEFITS of using your product or service. Don't assume people already know — they don't!

6. **Show off those pearly whites!**

   Display a picture of you or your team somewhere on the site. Customers trust levels increase when you appear *"more human."* Real photos are important. We all know when we're looking at some fake stock photo of a pretty girl.

7. **Never forget SEO (Search Engine Optimization).**

   Search Engine Optimization means optimizing your site so that when someone types a keyword into Google (or any search engine), your site comes up on the first page. You need to ensure every word possible on your site helps people find you on search engines. For example, type in *"postcard marketing"* in Google and PostcardMania is in the search results. Remember, people searching for your product or service already want it... don't neglect them!

8. **Put in time behind the scenes... and get with the program.**
The coding and programming for your site are vitally important, though nobody can see them. Well-programmed sites can improve your search engine rankings and allow you to easily update your content. It's important that the person you hire to program your site is a professional that is up to date on the latest technology.

9. **Get their contact info.**
Placing a fill-in form on your site is an easy way to get a new lead's contact info. People won't give it away for free, so offer a free report or exclusive web coupon in exchange for at least their email and name (address and phone number are bonuses!).

10. **DON'T BE CHEAP!**
Your website is not something you want to cut corners on! Your nephew who *"knows computers"* is not the man for the job. You need a website development company that offers the following services:
   • Web Design
   • Marketing Savvy
   • SEO
   • Copywriting
   • Programming

Your website is the link to a multitude of prospects that may be researching your product or service online. You need to make an impression and create awareness that your business exists. Again, over 95% of your mailing list that is interested will visit your website before calling or coming into your location — so it's important to make a good impression with professional web design.

19

INTEGRATING WITH ONLINE MARKETING

So you've got direct mail postcards and all this new-fangled internet technology, but how do you integrate them to get the most for your money?

Interesting you should ask, because actually using both mediums WILL get you the best results, and I just so happen to know how to do it. The key is to be in control of the process. This is how to do it...

Step by Step: Guiding Your Leads to a Sale

Here is a card that we sent. It has one central message: get your first 5,000 postcards free. Then it has one simple call to action, visit postcardmania.com/dentalfree.

Example Marketing Postcard

Step One - Postcard

- Simple copy
- Bullet points to quickly communicate
- Immediately directs reader to next step: the landing page

Each step is designed to get the prospect to take one more step. The postcard is designed to get the prospect to go to the landing page.

Example Landing Page

Step Two - Landing Page

- Bullet point the report's benefits

Once they're there, they can easily see what to do. That is our lead generation. We now have the contact info of a person who is interested in doing direct mail and we can follow up with them. This gives us a much hotter person to follow up with than just any general person on the mailing list.

Example Thank You Page

Step Three - Thank You Page

Okay, so now we have our *"lead."* We're done, right? Campaign success? Not even close! When a prospect fills out the form and hits the button, where do they go?

Well, think about what you know about them. For us, we know the person is interested in doing direct mail.

Then, we look for a way to combine what we know about the prospect with what is best for us. How do we create the win-win situation? The answer is simple — we route them to a page that thanks them for their information and prompts them to call in for immediate assistance. We know they're looking for answers, and the best way for us to help them is to get them connected — live — with someone who has those answers.

It's a step-by-step process and you have to follow through! Don't get a nibble and think you've landed the big one. Set the hook and reel them in with a great landing page — and don't stop until you've made them a customer!

CAMPAIGNING AND TRACKING

In this section you will learn:

- How to put together a successful direct mail campaign
- How to effectively use repetition in your marketing
- How to track your successful campaign

20

EVERYWHERE SMALL BUSINESS

―――――

So I have laid out proven principles for generating consistent results with direct mail. And I have talked about the importance of marketing integration (e.g. using different marketing strategies to generate leads and turn them into sales). And if you're thinking that all this just sounds like a bit too much to handle, especially for a small business owner without a dedicated marketing professional on staff...Well, you're right! It should!

There is a lot to handle — too many hats for just one head, if you will.

Enter Everywhere Small Business®
Everywhere Small Business® is the groundbreaking, industry-shaking product. Basically, instead of just ordering a direct mail campaign (design, printing, mailing, etc.), you can now get a

completely integrated campaign that includes:

- Postcard Design
- Mailing List Acquisition
- Printing
- Addressing & Mailing Services
- Mail Tracking
- Automatic Online Follow-up
- Phone Response Tracking

Imagine this: You're super excited about your new postcard campaign, because you have the perfect design and a mailing list that targets only the highest quality prospects. You are itching to know when they will actually reach mailboxes. So you log into your Everywhere Small Business® (aka ESB) account and easily find out the exact date the cards will be delivered. Simple!

Now imagine this: one of your ideal prospects gets your card and goes to your website for more information. Yes! But then they leave your site without filling out a contact form or calling you. Noooo!

But have faith — they're actually not lost, because ESB kicks in and starts to show follow-up banner ads to the prospects who bail on your site without interacting. And I'm talking about banner ads on MILLIONS of websites worldwide, from CNN.com to HGTV.com. Eventually, the prospect clicks one of the ads to return to your site and complete the purchase. YAHTZEE!

Noooow, imagine this: You are swamped with new business, but you don't know how much is attributable to the postcards. What to do? It's easy actually. You just log into your ESB account and get a full report on how many calls you received from the mailing AND how many online prospects your campaign is still following!

I know I sound excited — because I am! At the time of writing this, we've seen results from thousands of clients and their ROI is so much better than with direct mail alone. I've got a case study for you to review at the end of this chapter.

Let's break down how Everywhere Small Business® helps you maximize response with minimal effort:

Step 1: Direct Mail Acts as Your Lead Generator
Direct mail postcards are a proven lead generator for small businesses. They are effective because of all the reasons outlined in the previous chapters of this book (i.e. targeted mailing lists, no envelope to open, reach large audiences, etc.). And you are using them already, so no need to belabor the point here.

Step 2: Mail Tracking Keeps You Prepared to Succeed
Now, when your postcards get mailed, it benefits you to know when they will reach your prospects, because as your cards begin to generate responses, you need to be ready to handle those responses. Of course, you ideally want to prepare to handle the influx in the most cost-efficient manner possible — and that's where mail tracking comes in. Mail tracking allows you to make the necessary preparations at the right time (i.e. when your prospects have received your card in their mailbox.) This way you don't waste money on extra staff or other preparations if the cards are held up in the mail.

Step 3: Your ESB Campaign Follows Up with Online, Facebook & Instagram ads.

If a prospect calls in to your business or fills out a form on your website, you know how to follow up (or you will once you read the follow-up chapter of this book!). But what if the prospect goes to your website and DOESN'T leave contact info? We've all done it, right? You are interested in a business, you go to their site, mosey around a bit and then leave. It happens a lot.

But when your prospects do it, how are you supposed to follow up with them? Everywhere Small Business® includes a tool that lets you track every prospect AND automatically show them targeted ads on millions of websites, plus on Facebook and Instagram, once they leave (if they don't convert from a visitor to a lead, of course). All you have to do is include a small portion of code on your website and design your ads (and we can do all that). The process happens automatically from there.

Of course, you still don't have their name and email address, but it's the next best thing. The prospect will be exposed to your message by seeing your ad literally hundreds or even thousands of times, eventually getting them to click back through to your website or call you.

This creates brand awareness and credibility for you, and gives you the same tools the gigantic companies use. I'm sure you've noticed this when you visit a big site and then leave — their ads are everywhere! Well, that will be YOUR company with Everywhere Small Business®.

Step 4: Call Tracking Helps You Improve with Each New Campaign

ESB lets you see how effective your campaign is at creating callers. If you have a product or service that requires the prospect to actually speak with someone at your company in order to become a customer, you definitely want to ensure the postcard and the follow-up ads get people to actually pick up that phone and call. ESB lets you track exactly how many people are calling in using a call tracking feature that gathers data from your phone responses.

A unique phone number is used to route calls to your office, but it also counts how many responses come in from each campaign. The software even records your phone calls, so you can evaluate your reception and sales tactics. This data allows you to experiment with different designs, messages, and offers to find which combination gets the best response.

When all is said and done: if you are a business owner who doesn't have the time or staff to effectively set up, monitor, and tweak a complete marketing campaign, ESB can save you a ton of time, hassle, and money. It is not my intention to proselytize in this book (you can definitely purchase all of these services separately and handle them yourself). But my mission is to make marketing easier on you — not more complex.

Case Study

Kathleen Mullaney, DDS, FAGD

Kathleen Mullaney, DDS, FAGD Marketing Postcard

Length of Time Mailing Postcards:

Dr. Mullaney has been mailing 12,000 postcards every month since 2019 with ESB, taking only two months off from mailings at the very beginning of the Covid-19 mandatory shutdowns for dentists.

Problem Trying to Solve:

Dr. Mullaney saw a big drop in her new patient numbers around 2009, and while another marketing agency initially helped boost those numbers, things had started to decline again. She knew her marketing approach needed another revamp. She attended our bi-annual Small Business Owners Growth Summit and came away with several big ideas to jump-start her marketing and her business.

ROI:

Following their first year of mailings with PostcardMania, they brought in over $145,000 from new patients responding to her postcards, and, as of the beginning of 2021, Dr. Mullaney directly attributes 26 new patients to her postcard campaign.

As a high-end boutique practice that is fee-for-service (meaning they don't accept any type of insurance), Dr. Mullaney calls this *"wildfire kind of good."* The lifetime value of each of her patients is $8,500 to $9,500, which puts her return somewhere between $221,000 on the low end and $247,000 on the higher end of that spectrum. At the time I spoke with her, she had spent $39,261.30 on her campaign, which puts her ROI around 462% to 529%.

Now let's talk about how to budget for your marketing. *(Hint: There is a worksheet that makes it super simple.)*

21

HOW MUCH TO MAIL

Most novice marketers have definite fixed ideas about direct mail that are way off base — most often in the area of what to spend and how much to mail. Without enough marketing, one might experience a continuous *"failure"* in the area and really begin to believe their efforts are in vain. It has always been my belief that you should determine what you are able to spend for your marketing budget, spend it and determine the maximum number of leads you can create.

With that said, I have to admit I hear this statement quite often: *"We aren't a large company. How could we send out 5,000 postcards at once?"*

I totally understand this question, because *"What if they **all** call?"* seems like a valid concern, right?

Here is the reality behind it: Unfortunately, they won't all call. However, a good deal of them very well may and making sure your traffic is not more than you can handle is something to think about.

Truthfully, there is no sure way to tell exactly how many people will call if you haven't done this type of marketing before. Think of it this way: what would happen if they did all call? You may not be able to handle all of them, but you would handle as many as you possibly could, right?

In this scenario, you would have maximized your income for that time period, providing you close up all those callers! You can also explore the idea of expanding your operation to handle the number of leads you can create.

What if you don't max out your promotion at the very start? You can afford to send 4,000 pieces every two weeks, but you think you will simply get too many calls to be able to handle. So instead, you send out 2,000 and the response is decent. However, you still have downtime and find yourself trying to manufacture sales.

You saved $800 in marketing money, but you had enough downtime to close quite a few more sales. The question now becomes, *"Which gives me more money in my pocket? Saving $800 on marketing, or closing more sales and earning a few thousand dollars?"*

More than likely the answer is to spend as much as you possibly can on your marketing, right? By spending all that you can afford on marketing when you start a program, you maximize your income almost immediately.

The scenarios above are interesting, but not common. Most folks are concerned with not getting enough leads, not too many. The question I hear most often is, *"What if I send out 5,000 postcards, shell out $2,000 of my hard-earned money (postage is about $1,400 of that $2,000 by the way) — and* **nobody** *calls?"*

You will never know which scenario will occur for you without actually doing a mailing. I promise you one thing: if you apply all the things you learn in this manual, you won't have zero incoming leads from your postcard marketing efforts.

But how many leads should you expect? Good question. And it's a very common one. People want to know what they can expect. This something else I hear all the time:

"Okay, I'm on board. I'll send out 5,000 postcards. What will my response be like?"

You know what I say? *"How the heck should I know?"*

I can't possibly know for sure. There are a ton of variables in every campaign. How much competition do you have? Do they market regularly?

But the truth is, it's different for different industries, different postcards, different lists, different promotions and even different times of the year.

This is not a turnkey industry where you plug in a formula, fill in a blank, pull the trigger on the mailing and reap exactly what any salesperson told you to expect. Besides, there really is a saner way to look at it than number of responses versus number of pieces sent out.

ROI or Return On Investment

Let's talk about ROI — Return On Investment. With 5,000 postcards sent, you're spending about $2,000 total ($1,400 on postage). First of all, you need to track the responses very carefully in order to see the number of leads that come in off of a specific mailing, and how many of those actually closed. What is the amount of money you earned after spending the initial $2,000? This is your ROI. At my company, when a customer doesn't get the results they expected, we go down a checklist with them to help them figure it out.

You can ask yourself these same questions:
- Is the list I used for the right market/audience?
- Is the list I used fresh?
- Did the design have a bold headline and a bold color scheme?
- Did I list the benefits of the product/service on the back?
- Did I tell the recipient to call or go to my website with my postcard copy?
- Did my receptionist route all the leads?
- Is my receptionist reliable?
- Did I track them to see how many actually came in?

The Myth of the Bad Receptionist: A Marketing Fable

I can't tell you how many times it has been *"lousy receptionist"* as the *"why"* behind the *"no leads"* complaint. This next thing really has nothing to do with this particular manual, but I'd feel remiss if I didn't mention it.

Your receptionist is the first living, breathing line into your business. He or she is more than the mere gatekeeper to your sales people and production staff; she is equal parts customer service rep, den mother, big sister, cheerleader, tour guide and bouncer!

Of course, you can always use a computer-generated service to answer your calls, but why would you? Those things are evil!

Do you like it when a machine picks up when you're calling a business for the first time? Do you hit zero over and over until a living person picks up? Do you hate it when that living person sounds like a zombie and like they couldn't care less if you reached the person you're trying to reach? Have I made my point?

Unfortunately, business people assume the best receptionist is one who works for low wages. Why would you pay low wages for the first impression your company makes?

We always have a living, breathing receptionist. As we expanded our business over time and the number of incoming calls grew and grew, we found that our leads started to flatline. We were sending out more and more postcards, but we weren't getting a higher amount of leads. We discovered that many of the calls — about 200 a day — were going directly to our voicemail.

We decided to hire a second receptionist to answer the phones along with our regular receptionist. What happened? You guessed it. The leads picked right back up.
And the number of incoming calls in general skyrocketed. Prior, about 200 a day went to voicemail, but even more had

simply hung up and we could never know how many leads we actually missed.

Never underestimate the human factor in doing business. Postcard design, campaigning, tracking, it's all for naught if your prospects can't feel the human factor behind the message you give them — and the service they get. So in discussing what you should expect from your mailing, you must take into consideration ALL factors involved, especially the human factor.

I have to tell you another story: this time about a company that mailed solely on blind faith and just refused to track the responses. What kind of person would spend postage money month after month after month without tracking results? Who in this world would follow my advice religiously without question? My husband, of course.

His entire industry had changed dramatically. (He does title searches and document retrieval for mortgage lenders and title companies.) He, along with all his colleagues, found themselves with half the business they had the previous year. He has four really close friends that all do the same thing, but are in different territories around the country. They're always comparing numbers — number of new orders in, dollar value of that number, gross income, etc.

Anyway, when his numbers crashed back in April of 2004, I basically told him it's *"do or die"* time. Then, a year and two months after the first mailing, he hit a highest-ever month in his company's six-year history. And after checking with his friends, they were still suffering with low numbers and complaining about the industry in general.

So what's the secret? Well, it's only a *"secret"* if you just flipped to this page and started reading! He mails 12,000 cards, month after month, like clockwork. We designed a series of cards and over this period he's built great credibility with his potential client base. But I also have to say that he is a brilliant executive and really delivers a superb product with terrific customer service, too. Postcards can generate leads, but you have to be able to close the sale and deliver the product if you want to succeed. It all comes back to the human element; no business can succeed without it.

What is his ROI? Well, with no mailings his company brought in $80,000 in April 2004 — a total crash. The next year he did upwards of $180,000. The gross income started going up immediately after he started the mailings. He tracked nothing but his income and his new orders. He still mails and in 2014 his company grossed about $500,000 per month. Update 2022 — his company now grosses $900,000 on average per month.

We have no idea how many reaches into his company there were. We have no idea of the number of new customers. We know none of those things. But we do know he's making way more income. If he didn't have friends to compare numbers with, one might simply say, *"Well, the industry is turning around — thank goodness."* But this would be a false *"why."* He's marketing consistently and he's bringing in more income. Period. In the above example, he was spending around $4,000 per month on postcard mailings and his income went up $100,000 per month.

Do you think that is a good ROI? I sure do.

Your Formula for Your Business

With my husband Sam's business, we chose a random amount of cards to start mailing. We did this because he wasn't doing ANY marketing at the time and we knew that a good amount to send for acquiring new business is about 10,000 pieces per month. We have started many companies off with this amount and it always pays off if done consistently. But, there is a more organized and mathematical way to figure this out if you're up for it:

1. **Do a test mailing of 5,000 pieces.**
   This is the number I recommend for a successful test mailing, based on nearly two decades of experience.

2. **Ensure all points for a good design are included in the piece (covered in Chapter 14.)**
   If necessary, re-read. (In fact, I'd make that mandatory!) Put a promo code on the postcards so that you can track the responses. Without this code, tracking will be twice as difficult — and half as effective. Or use Everywhere Small Business® and tracking will be automatic.

3. **Gather information using the human factor if you don't have auto tracking in place.**
   You'll have to have your sales rep or receptionist ASK, *"How did you hear about us?"* If *"postcard"* is the answer, then proceed with the next question: *"Can you give me that marketing code you see there on your postcard, please?"* Of course with call tracking, this won't be necessary and there will be no human error.

4. **Keep track of all incoming data.**

    Take note of all responses and where they came from, regardless of whether or not you think they're qualified (someone unqualified today may become qualified down the road — never disregard an incoming lead).

5. **After about four weeks, evaluate how many leads you closed off of that mailing.**

    I have to tell you, though: "*four weeks*" is completely arbitrary. Obviously, different businesses have different sales cycles. Some products are easily sold with one phone call, while others require much more follow-up. But this is a good place to start. Leads will actually continue to straggle in over time as well. Truthfully, if you want to email me, I can help you figure out what works as a test for your industry: joy.gendusa@postcardmania.com.

6. **Figure out what additional income you brought in due to that test mailing.**

    This would be impossible without proper tracking procedures, so if you haven't done step 4, go back and start over.

7. **At this point, you want to come up with how much additional income you would like to make.**

    For instance, let's say you made an additional $10,000 that month over what you normally make, but you'd be happier with an extra $20,000. Well, if 5,000 cards yielded $10,000 up to this point, then you can safely assume that 10,000 pieces will yield double that.

8. **Read the next chapter on campaigns.**

   There is very valuable data in there on how all of this works. I developed a worksheet, provided in this chapter, to figure out your mailing formula. But in order to know exactly how much you'll need to send in order to yield the results you want, you'll have to test mail and then mail consistently. The main thing is to never give up.

9. **Keep mailing no matter what.**

   When and if your sales numbers slow down, mail even more in order to make up for it. If you stop mailing, your leads will dry up and result in even lower sales.

I have a little story for you in regards to #9 above. When COVID-19 hit, we had an instant drop in business of 40%. Super scary when you have 300 employees to pay. I made the tough decision to pay only two bills each week — my marketing (an internal bill) and my payroll. Period. In 5 weeks, we recovered fully AND ended 2020 10% up over 2019.

Why? I never cut my marketing. But my competitors ALL did. I have other similar stories in my 23 years doing this — times that were slower or expansion expenses higher, where logically (it seemed) that cutting a percentage of my marketing budget would be best for the time being. One time I did do that — and my revenue followed. I will never do that again.

22

SCHEDULING YOUR CAMPAIGNS

Our bodies can't travel to the future, but our minds sure can — and they should if you want to run a successful direct marketing campaign. So when planning your business marketing strategy, start thinking about your Valentine's Day promotion or your Fourth of July promotion early — very early. Say — on the day before Thanksgiving.

When scheduling your promotions, it's kind of like a game of chess: **You should always be thinking at least three moves ahead.**

In this case, each *"move"* should be one month. Therefore, you should be thinking about your Valentine's or February promotions as you fall asleep after your big turkey dinner. There are a few reasons why you need to have your promotions figured out that early. Getting direct mail out the door to the post office and into the hands of your prospects TAKES TIME.

By having it all worked out months in advance, you give yourself enough time for the logistics. Getting the concept down, figuring out your offer, getting artwork put together, printing, and mailing all have to be done — and this can take several weeks from being an idea in your head to being a piece of promo in your customers' hands. You are also going to want to have the piece in your customers' hands at least two weeks before the sale or event, so be sure to factor in this time as well.

Get the Message Out Multiple Times
Repeat, repeat, repeat. You need TIME if you want your list to get at least three mailings, right? Getting your postcards out early lets you drive your message home through repetition.

Take the December holidays, for example. If you start mailing to your customers in the beginning of November, you will be able to cement your company name in their heads because you will be able to mail to them multiple times before they have to make their holiday purchases.

On the other hand, if you start mailing to them in late November or early December, you will not have the time to do multiple mailings. Nevertheless, getting one mailing out at that stage will still be much better than not sending anything at all. However, nothing works better when promoting than multiple mailings with the same message to the same list.

In this life, there are three kinds of people:
- Those who show up early
- Those who arrive on time
- Those who get there late

Now, we are all given the same 24 hours in a day. But clearly the people who show up early use theirs more effectively. Where do you fall on this list? Chances are, if you are the type of person who shows up on time or even late, then so will your postcards. So learn to manage your time better to get those cards out earlier.

Keep a calendar and flip ahead. The minute you finish one mailing, schedule the next. Always make sure to stay three moves ahead — or three months ahead of the season. This way you'll always be early!

Free Up Time to Run Your Business
Most people who own a business do their own marketing. Thankfully, marketing is one of the few things in a business that you can do far in advance. By scheduling your holiday promotions ahead of time (consult your calendar!), you will make yourself available to do all of the other jobs your business requires of you.

Scheduling promotions can seem like a huge task, but some things are just worth the extra thought. Think back to the calendar idea. When you really get down to brass tacks, it really isn't that daunting. After reading this manual, you will truly be an expert and, once your scheduling is done, you'll have time to put your ideas and energy into other areas that need your attention so you can maximize your efforts toward expansion.

I find the easiest way to plan in advance is to go backward. So let's go back to our last section and pick up where we left off: Get a calendar; either a day planner or the kind with a box for each date/day or even the one on your laptop or iPad works great. First, you're going to choose the *"hit date,"* meaning the date you want your list to actually receive your postcard in their mailbox.

On that date on the calendar write *"Mail Hits."* Next, go four days back in time on the calendar (not including Sunday or a national holiday, as the Post Office is closed those days). On that date write *"mail drop"* — meaning this is the day your mail house is to drop the postcards at the Post Office.

Following is a seven-point list. By writing each of these on a date, you can control when your mail will hit and thus begin the process of predicting results — and income:

1. Choose target market and get mailing list count
2. Place order for quantity needed. (1 & 2 can be done the same day in most cases)
3. Design and layout complete and approved
4. Printed product complete
5. Lists processed and postage paid
6. Mail addressed and dropped at the post office
7. Mail hits homes and businesses

JANUARY						
S	M	T	W	T	F	S
1	2	**1** 3	**2** 4	5	6	7
8	9	10	**3** 11	12	13	14
15	16	17	**4** 18	**5** 19	20	21
22	23	**6** 24	25	26	27	28
29	**7** 30	31				

Calendar showing a typical postcard marketing turnaround time.

When choosing a company to work with, make sure they know you have a deadline and your intention is to get these points done on these specific dates.

Ensure they are in agreement and it can be done. I highly recommend NOT rushing. Why? When you put a lot of stress on creative types, when you completely stress them out with a major RUSH job, you won't get the best they can do.

At our company, we guarantee three to five business days for a full conceptual design to be delivered for approval. This is considered rather fast, but we've found through experience that it still gives the designer time to research and come up with a brilliant idea.

So, make use of that calendar and give yourself time to do it right. It will be worth it in the end.

23

REPETITION IS EVERYTHING.
REPETITION IS EVERYTHING.

———

Kids are instinctive about something I like to call *"The Rule of Repetition."* It's a marketing secret that every child knows — and you should, too. In its least scientific — but most effective — form, The Rule of Repetition sounds a little something like this: *"Mom, Mom, Mom, Mom, can I have an ice cream? Can I? Can I? Can I? Can I? Please. Please. Please. Please. I'll be good for a whole year. I promise. Just give me a dollar. I won't ask again for a looooooooooong time. Pleaseeeeeee!"* And if you happen to be a fan of The Big Bang Theory — Sheldon knocking on Penny's door, *"Penny, Penny, Penny, Penny, Penny."*

What can we learn from a child's insistent urging for an ice cream — or a bicycle or a doll or a teddy bear or a skateboard or to stay up late? Plenty. In fact, The Rule of Repetition will be one of your biggest allies as you move forward toward your first postcard marketing campaign. That is because **regular, repeated mailings** are the best way to create **big, predictable results**. When you mail every 30 days for a year, you will cause a dramatic growth in your business. I'll repeat that: When you mail every 30 days for a year, you will cause a dramatic growth in your business.

The Rule of Repetition states that people respond to repetition. If you are a parent, or have ever been on the same line with one in the grocery store aisles, you know how hard it is to refuse repeated requests for an ice cream cone or a desperately wanted toy. Why not welcome this rule into your life by applying it to your very own marketing campaign?

Repetition In Your Campaign

Many people ask me, *"What is a postcard campaign, exactly? And do I really need one?"*

My answer is always the same: *"Only if you want to sell something!"*

The postcard campaign is to direct marketing what the gas tank is to your next road trip: fuel for the journey — and the only way to get from Point A to Point B. Unfortunately, this strategy is also the hardest part of the process to teach.

It's not as simple as showing a postcard design or handing over a mailing list; campaigns require patience and persistence in order to pay off. And yet no matter how hard I try or how much proof I give, people just don't want to believe it. But I owe you the truth. For the money you spent on this manual, you deserve nothing but the truth.

So here goes. First, a quick definition:

cam • paign /kam pān/ n.
1. A series of military operations undertaken to achieve a large-scale objective during a war. *Ex: Grant's Vicksburg campaign secured the entire Mississippi for the Union.*
2. An operation or series of operations energetically pursued to accomplish a purpose. *Ex: An advertising campaign for a new product; a candidate's political campaign.*

As you might have guessed, the second definition is the one we're using.

Campaigns for marketing are, in a nutshell, a series of advertising steps, including repeat mailings, strategically planned to attain maximum benefit (more new customers) for your business.

Note: If you are not doing repeat mailings, you are flushing money down the toilet. Sorry, I know. The truth sometimes hurts.

Why is this true? One mailing of one postcard one time is barely going to get anyone's attention for more than the one minute (or one second) they see it. Think about it. How many times have you seen the same TV commercials, over and over?

They are appealing to The Rule of Repetition, which states the more often a prospect sees something, the more likely they are to become a customer. You'll notice there is no Rule of Restriction here! That's because (usually) a single shot-in-the-dark postcard mailing is not going to change your business, your bottom line, your life or anything.

So, if you are not up to confronting the fact that you need a campaign, maybe you shouldn't be in business. That may sound harsh — because it is harsh. It's a harsh world.

And I want you to succeed in it. It's better that I'm harsh now and show you the right way than life being harsh later — after you've spent thousands on a single mailing cop-out and NOT a campaign.

There is another reason The Rule of Repetition makes campaigns a necessity, not a luxury — credibility. In some cases, people will hold onto your postcard for a while. They can hold onto your postcard for six months. They may even hold on to your card for three years. But in most cases they'll think, *"Oh, I may need that someday"* and then while tidying up they'll throw it away. When you repeat your mailings to those same people and they see your image, logo, slogan and message over and over, you become credible to them. Your chances of them responding just got greater — in a big way.

The U.S. Small Business Administration reports that 49% of new businesses fail within five years. Why is that? Simply put, they don't have enough people paying money to them for their services. The bottom line is, they don't market. Therefore, they don't get people buying their stuff. That's the whole point of marketing.

Yes, of course, some promotion is better than no promotion. And sending out a one-time mailing is better than never sending any mailing at all. But this is a chapter about campaigns, not complaints. With a real campaign of repeat mailings, you will soon learn to predict your growth.

Eventually, you will see trends within your own company based on specials or offers on your postcards. You'll know which offers pull more responses. And if you keep track of how much income comes off of each promotion, you'll be better able to predict the results of your next mailing. That means you can personalize your strategy — create **your campaign** based on **your results**.

Let's keep it simple: **Your income is dependent upon how often your message is communicated to your target list**; the more prospects that see your message, the more income you'll make. After some time of mailing consistently, you will know how much you need to mail in order to bring in the desired dollar amount to give you enough of a return on investment.

If you put out a blast of communication, you will get inflow — prospects and customers calling or coming in and buying. If you're one of the small businesses still surviving on referrals, you are an extreme rarity these days. Yes, delivering a good product gets you some business from referrals, but only some. You want to blast repeatedly to get consistent inflow. And consistency is where prediction comes in. You could almost make a big flow chart of what will happen.

For instance: say you send out 5,000 postcards.
- Out of that 5,000, 150 hang onto your postcard.
- Out of that 5,000, so many call the first week.
- Out of that 5,000, so many call the second week.
- Out of that 5,000, so many call the next month.
- Out of that 5,000, so many call in 6 months.
- Out of that 5,000, so many never call...

As you can clearly see, there is a dwindling inflow from that first mailing and therefore can give a false impression of what occurs from one mailing. Someone sends out a postcard and says, *"I only got four responses from my mailing!"* But there is a whole dynamic going on from that one mailing after the business owner who sent the mailing expects things to happen.

Think about it this way: Do you jump at every single advertisement that seems like a good deal? If you do, you are either a gazillionaire or broke. Most likely, an advertisement catches your interest and you say to yourself *"I'd like to check that out someday."* Then, you see it again and remember you wanted to *"check that out"* one day. Then, you see it again and this time you decide to actually check it out. Or you file it away and when you pay off that credit card, pull it out and visit the store that advertised the rug you wanted for your living room.

Victoria's Secret, Pottery Barn, Harry & David (and any reputable catalog company) will mail you catalogs not just once, but multiple times! Are you getting the picture yet? How many Pottery Barn catalogs have you received without ever making a purchase? And yet they keep sending them.

Do you think even a company as big as Pottery Barn or Victoria's Secret has enough money to consistently waste it sending out catalogs to people if they didn't think they would eventually buy something? These companies have the smartest minds in marketing working for them and even so, it still all boils down to one thing: The Rule of Repetition.

You want continuous and consistent growth. So what do you do? Look at this scenario: What if...

- You send out 5,000 postcards one week and you have everything going on I mentioned in the earlier flow chart from above.
- You send out 5,000 the next week and you have everything going on I mentioned above.
- You send out 5,000 the next week with the dwindling flow chart going on for each one of those outflows — turning those outflows to inflows.

What is going to happen? Hmmmm, let me see: Eventually, it is going to snowball — it's coming in from all different places! You are really putting your communication out there consistently and in a big way. You are following The Rule of Repetition and making the most out of your campaign.

I'll be the first one to admit it costs a lot of money to do it. (Once you have your list, which you'll use over and over, postage is more than 55% of your costs.)

So, FIND THE MONEY.

Say it with me, *"FIND THE MONEY!"* If you are going to borrow money to run a business, spend it wisely. In other words, spend that borrowed money on marketing!

This is the thing about capital investment: People get money to start their business, but often they don't prioritize properly. They give themselves a nice big salary; they buy really great furniture, computers, rent a great office, etc. That's not where they should be spending the bulk of their money. They should be spending their money on marketing and promotion and getting their name out there. Then — and only then — the money coming in from sales can be spent on upgrading computers or designing a fabulous office.

Then and only then.

But I digress; back to campaigns and mailing every week: Start with a list and mail to one list one week, another list the next week and another list the following week. Then, rotate those lists again and again and again.

You might be asking, *"What if you only have one list?"* You can still rotate one list — by dividing it up. Take that one list and divide it up into a series of smaller lists. (Naturally, it is always good to put it in a spreadsheet or a flow chart to track what you are doing and what you have already done.)

For instance: You get one list of 6,000 identities; now split it into thirds. You can mail to 2,000 one week, 2,000 the next week and 2,000 the third week. Then you rotate. There are your three different lists!

Okay, okay, you got the point. The next thing to know about campaigns is the two different types of marketing campaigns:

There is the campaign to get your customers to keep buying from you so they don't go elsewhere — and then there is the campaign to get new business in.

Once you have gotten new business in, then those customers (that once were prospects) get the repeat-customer campaign.

Where Do You Start?
Priorities Before Pencil Holders

When you have a problem or need a favor, the first people you turn to are those in your immediate circle, right? Your family, friends, neighbors and colleagues.

Well, why should your customers feel left out? The first thing you should do when thinking of a marketing campaign is to start with your own customers.

Say you've been in business 5–10 years and have hit a plateau; start by mailing out to your own customers that have been with you and already know you are good.

And then, once you get your income up a little bit, start the second campaign to market to new customers.

Be smart with your money; prioritize. Finding the money is often as easy as looking right under your own nose. Look at your last bank statement and highlight the luxuries.

Cigarettes, movies, books, CDs, bar tabs, Twinkies! These are the quickie items you can cut out immediately. But don't stop there; keep right on going. Don't go out for dinner quite as much.

Don't buy that new Lexus (yet)!

Don't invest in that piece of real estate right now. Put your money back into your business. If you prioritize wisely, you might be able to tackle two campaigns at once!

If you have made all your money with your business, then that business is the goose that is laying the golden egg (for the eventual Lexus), so put money back in your business first. Go ahead and spend the newly earned money on both the customer retention campaign (Campaign #1) and finding new customers (Campaign #2).

Sure, be selfish and spend the money you need on things you want — you've earned it, but just be patient. Wait until your marketing is really paying off and you couldn't stop the influx of business if you tried before you take from your professional account to spend on the personal. Above, I am speaking to someone that has gotten very comfortable in their own income and doesn't necessarily want to cut their own income to grow their business. But if you have a new business and really only have twelve customers, then you have to do a campaign to get new customers.

And it costs money; it will be a big expense.

So prioritize where you can and save where you must. For instance, buy a used computer. Most of the $10,000 you borrowed from your dad — or maxed out on your credit cards — to start up your new business should be spent on marketing, not the latest promotion from Dell or Mac. Work out of your bedroom on a used computer, then sell and deliver your product or service. When you've sold plenty, then you pay yourself (when Dad's paid off and you actually have money, that is).

And just to let you know — I'm not asking you to do anything I didn't do or anything I'm not doing currently. Everything in this manual has been proven out by my personal experience and observing the results of tens of thousands of customers.

Build Your Marketing Campaign and They Will Come
Postcard campaigns are a lot like postcard designs. The bare minimum will work, but why stop there? A campaign could be as simple as mailing the same postcard over and over again to the same list. You'd still be campaigning if you did it this way — and you would have results.

However, you could get closer and closer to your ideal results with a *"several-different-messages"* campaign. You could design each piece so that it communicates to different types of people. For instance, FEAR is a common feeling for people when they are about to make a purchase. You could use this universal emotion to make your cards communicate how safe it would be to try your product or service — or how awful it could be for them if they don't. There's one card down. Maybe for your second card you offer a money back guarantee. People also respond to humor. A third card in your campaign could be funny. Different folks will respond to different emotions in advertising, and this way you are able to reach them all with a unique message.

A VERY successful way to put together a campaign is to create a series of cards mailed one after the other with some time in between to your market. All of these postcards should look similar. Not the same, but similar. You could do a three-card, four-card, five-card campaign. The look and feel should match, meaning your logo is in the same place each time, your color scheme is the same, etc.

Again, planning is key here; you have to come up with your look and feel beforehand. I suggest you design and mail the first one and check for results.

You can tweak it, but choose your basic colors FIRST. Do a little research. Which colors communicate to you the most? Be your own survey person. Love your mail piece. Don't sign off on anything a designer came up with if you don't love it. You'll imbue it with results. It'll pull better if you love it. Sounds nutty, but it's true. I talk a lot more about design in chapter 13, in case you skipped it.

One thing about campaigns is that you have to commit to a campaign. I mean really commit.

Wherever you buy your marketing services from, commit to a campaign. Let them design all five pieces at once. I don't suggest printing them all at once. Tweak the design on the others if you need to as you go, but definitely commit to the process and fulfill your commitment.

Consumers rarely get multiple postcards from a business. Yet it is such a brilliant system. When I receive multiple postcards, I take a look. I think, *"Hmmm, these guys are still contacting me."*

That shows persistence; it shows credibility. You are building credibility with a campaign. That is the point. So, hit 'em again, Sam.

A great movie had a great quote that is well-remembered but not necessarily true: *"build it and they will come."* Ever hear that? People think it means if you put a building there, people will come. Or they think if you build a website, people will automatically visit it. No, you have to drive customers to your business. So, *"build it and they will come"* should actually have been *"build your marketing campaign and they will come."* Because what you are building with a marketing campaign is credibility.

You are building your business through communication. You are communicating consistently, so people will believe you (credibility) and respond. They will come; they will spend.

Addendum

Everything I said years ago when I wrote this chapter is still true today in 2022. However, now you can exponentially increase your results by increasing the number of times your message is seen by your audience. And you don't have to do it all with postcards. Yes, you heard me right. Postcards are the differentiator. Your competitors are most likely only using online ads if they're marketing at all. By incorporating multiple channels into your campaign and having them all coincide and match each other, you can't help but be the biggest name in your industry in your area. And it's a lot easier than it sounds.

Imagine you create the perfect design that will go to the perfect list three times. Before that postcard hits mailboxes, those folks see ads matching your postcard in their Facebook feed and their Instagram feed. Then they get the card and might think, *"Mmmm, that's familiar to me and I'm interested."* They've already seen your offer several times. Once they go to your site — well it's all over. They'll now start seeing your ad over and over and over again.

Here's a great example. One of my clients, Dr. Amit Khanna of Patuxent Dental, completely turned his practice around using consistent postcard mailings coupled with online advertising.

The first three years in business, Dr. Khanna's revenue declined 14% overall. His marketing plan was virtually nonexistent — he had a homemade yard sign and ads in the yellow pages. His third year in business was his worst yet. He only collected $663,712 in revenue, down from $762,216 and $712,517 respectively.

By his fourth year in business, he knew he needed to do something to alter the course he found himself on. He tried postcards. His first campaign was a trial — just a few mailings of 6,000 cards here and there. But by the end of the year, revenue was way up — $825,409.

He was sold and started to mail 6,000 postcards every month. That year, he cracked a million and hit $1,280,568.

Then he decided to double his mailings to 12,000 every month and reached another highest-ever year at $1,451,707.

But he wasn't done yet! He worked with our team to coordinate digital ads with his mailings like I described above, and he hit these numbers the next three years:

- $2,152,052
- $2,640,261
- Over $3,000,000!

He managed to *more than double* his revenue by simply adding digital ads to his regular monthly mailings. That's the power of digital amplification.

24
◆ TRACK & TWEAK

How do you know your campaign is working? Some people just assume the card they like best is working — or the longest list is paying off with bigger profits. But that's assuming, not tracking. If you try to gauge results based on intuition versus information, it could cost you more than just the price of an ad campaign — it could cost you customers as well.

Tracking a campaign's results is a vital part of marketing and, frankly, can take your marketing campaign to a whole new plateau. So why don't more businesses do it?

Honestly — I have no idea. But they don't.

Like the example of sending out multiple cards to the same list in the earlier chapter, you have to know which ones are working and which aren't for them to be truly effective. Likewise, if you have more than one way to recruit new customers, you need to set up a tracking system so you know if each is working or not.

For example, you start a postcard marketing campaign for your business and send out 3,000 postcards the first week. When they start hitting homes, you get 30 calls. Did all of these leads come from the postcards? Probably not, because the week before you got 8 calls and hadn't sent out any postcards yet. So how can you tell who actually got a postcard?

The answer: All you have to do is ask them. It's as simple as asking, *"So how did you hear about our company?"* The hard part is making sure that any employee in your company who answers the phone and talks to a new prospect remembers to ask the question every time. (Give yourself this task and notice how many times YOU forget to ask. It's hard to create new habits and break old ones. So don't be too hard on your staff when they forget. Just gently remind them each day until the new habit is formed.) With that said, surveys increase in value with the number of participants.

Conversely, they suffer in value for lack of participants. So the fewer prospects that answer this question, the less accurate your information will be when making future marketing decisions.

Now, let's assume that you have been sending out postcards for a while and you have a good number of calls coming in. If you ask the question, *"So, how did you hear about our company?"* they may respond, *"I got your postcard in the mail."* But, by now you have mailed postcards to 4 different lists, 3 times each. That's a lot of variables to cover with such a simple Q & A. How do you tell which list — and which mailing — this customer was from?

One answer: Put a marketing code on the postcards that will tell you which specific postcard they received and when it was mailed.

Give each list a name and work the date into your marketing code as well. Now tracking comes into play, and the only thing your representatives have to ask is, "*Would you mind reading me the marketing code above your address?*" This code should give you all the info that you need to know to help you keep your marketing results tracking as accurate as possible.

Try not to operate off assumptions about what worked if you haven't tabulated your results. When you collect all the data, you can finally make your future marketing decisions based on the facts — not feelings.

That brings me to another tracking error.

As I've said before, one mailing at one time to one list is not going to change your bottom line. How long it takes for your particular market to make a decision (such as trying out what you have to offer) will determine how many times you should mail to them before deciding it's working or not working.

Wow. That was a mouthful. Let me try to unravel that.

I just spoke with a marketer who sent 20,000 pieces at one time to a list of bankruptcy attorneys. She got 3 or 4 responses. She decided it did not work. She tracked and that response is simply too low to produce the ROI she needs to make that a successful mailing. But, notoriously, lawyers do not move quickly or make rash decisions. What she should have done is send 3 mailings to a list of 7,000 attorneys and then determine her results. Now she's decided they won't respond and she is no longer mailing to them. However, those that were a bit interested will probably forget her if they don't get a reminder.

So my point is this — she tracked her response but didn't review ALL the data. How long does it take a lawyer to respond to a direct mail piece? That's not a riddle, just something to research if you've never mailed to lawyers before. OR, if doing that research isn't possible or feasible, practice effective repeat mailings before concluding it didn't work.

Tracking Made Easy
Does all of this tracking stuff sound like it's going to take forever to implement? Maybe like it's too much of a hassle to bother with? Well, guess what? I was holding out on you a little bit before, because I DO want you to get in the habit of asking every caller how they heard about you. It is a crucial tracking baseline to have.

But the truth is that there *is* a super simple way to track how many calls a postcard mailing generates: phone response tracking.

Phone response tracking comes standard with any Everywhere Small Business® campaign (refer back to Chapter 20 for details) and automatically tells you how many calls a specific campaign produced. It uses a different phone number for each postcard campaign (all of which forward to your main office number) and then compiles the call data for each number

in an easy-to-use format on your Everywhere Small Business®
digital dashboard. You just log in to monitor your campaign's
performance! You can even listen to every call because the
software automatically records them for you, which lets you
check your sales and reception staff for quality.

Tracking solved.

To Change or Not to Change...

I couldn't wrap up the advice in this book unless I put down the
last, but not least, important factor in monitoring your direct
mail marketing and your income. It has to do with when you
should change your marketing and what the tell-tale signs that
change is needed are. How does *"if it ain't broke, don't fix it"* apply
to marketing?

Change is good, right? Not always. Think about this: Why
would one take something that is going well — no, great — and
change it?

The obvious answer is to make it better, right? Not! In
business or in marketing, change is not always good.

When you have certain promotional actions that are in place
making things happen, or in better terms, making you money —
don't change them! Why do I say this? Because I see it time and
time again. Someone has a marketing campaign that is bringing
in a good return on investment and they up and decide to change
their postcard! And why do they do it? Believe it or not, this is the
answer I most often get, *"Er, uh, we just decided to do something
different."*

And then some three or four months down the road, they call back with their tail between their legs and want everything back the way it was before. In this latter case, change is good — changing it back to what was working.

I am not just saying that to say that one should always keep their postcard marketing campaign the same and never change it. Quite the contrary. Change your marketing, change your habits, change your way of life when it warrants it. There is really some truth to the old adage. *"If it ain't broke, don't fix it."* Maybe it's human nature to want to change everything once something gets going just the way they planned it. Who the heck knows? All I can say is step outside the human-nature box. Change only when things are drastic — or when change is warranted.

Drastic circumstances deserve drastic measures. But how do you determine drastic? Sometimes that is really easy. Your company's income is crashing. Do something! Change! Or better yet, figure out what you changed and get it back to what was working.

How about a plateau? Does that deserve change? Depends on how long that plateau lasts. I have never seen something level off and stay level forever. It either goes up or down.

I know an optometrist who had a very successful practice in Small Town, USA. He never really marketed. He never really had to. People knew of him from miles around. Mainly he did PR stuff — a fundraiser here, networking there, etc. His good works made him well known and respected and the community *"oooh'ed and ah'ed"* over him so much that the local newspaper paper loved printing it.

But things changed. Malls started opening up. People started shopping away from Small Town, USA and into the bigger cities and malls. The environment changed.

But he didn't. He still kept a good practice, but you could see something interesting — his gross income started to plateau. And over the years that plateau gradually started to show where it was really going. I'm sure you're getting the picture by now.

Now, would that demand drastic measures? Taking into account inflation, cost of living and other factors that are on the rise — yes, I would say that would demand drastic measures. Did he take them? Not until the dire nature of his situation became all too apparent. But yes, he finally did take them. He started postcard marketing his you-know-what off!

I have another client that is just a dream. They have had the same list for the past five years, ever since they have been in business, in fact. They mail to 30,000 physical therapists over and over and over and over and — and have never changed. They figure if it is bringing in the income, it is working. And it keeps working.

Marketing plans are like recipes; change one ingredient and the taste changes — sometimes for the better, sometimes for the worse. Remember how long it took you to create that recipe, how much testing and tasting and research and analysis went into creating a recipe specific to your company and your needs. Do you really want to go and mess with all that hard work and effort?

So, next time you think about changing your marketing plan, make sure it needs it. Look at your numbers. Are they improving?

Declining? If your income is going up — don't change one single thing. But if it is going down or flatlining — change!

25

FOLLOWING UP

How many leads have come into your business that did not close?

How many leads have come into your business since the beginning of time that never closed? I bet there are a lot.

Now think about these numbers oft-quoted by sales professionals:

- 2% of sales are made on the first contact.
- 3% of sales are made on the second contact.
- 5% of sales are made on the third contact.
- 10% of sales are made on the fourth contact.
- 80% of sales are made on the fifth to twelfth contact.

So... um... yeah. If you give up after 3 contacts, you could be leaving 75% of sales on the table! If you're not speechless, this is the part where you let a *"Golly gee whiz!"* slip. But it's still kinda tough to get your head around, right?

Let's look at an example:
- Postcard marketing experts tell you to send out 5,000 postcards
- It costs you $2,000 to send out those postcards
- You do that and you get 50 calls
- That cost is $40 per lead

Not bad. Now let's talk about Return On Investment (ROI). The ROI of this example is as follows:
- You make $2,000 off of every close.
- You close 20% out of those 50 calls (10 sales).
- You made $20,000.
- Take away the 2 grand for the postcards = $18,000.

That is decent ROI, but what about the 40 leads that never closed? That is $1,600 sitting out there on the table, spent with no return.

Now ask yourself, how many of your leads don't close per month? Take that theoretical situation and multiply $1,600 by the other 11 months. That is a chunk of change that you are basically blowing.

Don't get discouraged. Getting educated in marketing and determining your ROI is a major step in the right direction. Great ROI is what you should be going for, but don't stop there. There is more to sniff out.

So, what are you doing to get all of those that initially reached for your product or service?

How many phone calls do you make before you decide that a lead is unclosable? Zero... two... three? Did you leave a message on their voicemail and they didn't call back so you dropped them?

How many in a sales force are simply cherry-picking their leads, so to speak, and not closing or following up with the rest? How many of these dropped leads do you have built up? Can you see the waste?

You need to follow up. Even if you didn't get the ROI you anticipated or needed, you still need to follow up. But how? More specifically, what kind of campaign should you do to get even more ROI? Good question. Here's the answer.

First of all, realize that these prospects reached for you, your product or service and you CAN rehabilitate that initial interest. They are much easier to close and more valuable than someone who has never shown interest in your product or service before. Build on that.

For follow-up, it is extremely important to have a set schedule in place. So you should set up what's called a *"funnel"* system. The prospect will be contacted regularly over time through a variety of mediums.

For example:

- 1 day after call in: Added to follow-up postcard drip campaign list
- 1 day after call in: First email from follow-up email campaign
- 2 days after call in: Follow-up phone call
- 5 days after call in: Another follow-up call
- 7 days after call in: Second email from drip campaign
- 7 days after call in: Second postcard from drip campaign
- 9 days after call in: Third call attempt
- During all this time you NEVER stop feeding them ads on Facebook, Instagram and Google.

Again, that is just an example. You will need to tailor it to your business. Here is what should be involved:

Step One: Email Drip Campaign

Create a series of emails to go to your prospects at set intervals based on when they were added to your email list. This type of email campaign is called an *"Email Drip Campaign."*

It is set up to deliver emails automatically and can consist of as many emails and whatever time period you would like. The best way to set up a campaign like this is to use email marketing software. Do some research to find a company that fits your needs, but make sure they allow you to set up trigger-based emails (emails that get sent automatically when a certain *"trigger"* occurs).

Start with six messages where one message is sent to the email list each week for six weeks.

These emails are designed to warm up leads and get them interested enough to contact you again so you can sell to the easily.

Keep in mind, in order for this to be successful, you need to do everything you can to collect email addresses from your new leads and keep them current in your database and add these new leads to your drip campaign email list.

Every week, you should make sure all the new leads from that week have been added to the list to receive these emails.

Step Two: Email Newsletter

In addition to the email drip campaign, these prospects should receive a monthly email newsletter. You should be able to come up with a monthly email newsletter that would be appropriate for all of your prospects and clients. Each issue would contain new testimonials, news about what's happening at your company or in the industry, announcements about new staff members, but mostly helpful information about the solution your product or service provides that will assist the reader and be of value to them. If the newsletter is all about you and your company, it will be quickly deleted.

Step Three: Direct Mail

Implement a 3-postcard drip campaign for those prospects that contact you but don't close. These can be similar to your raw prospect postcards with the addition of something like, *"Thank you for your interest!"*

You'll need to have a mailing list specifically for these cards and update the list with all new prospects before you mail it each month. You will also need to then remove contacts from this list once they have become customers so you don't continue to ask a person to do something they've already done!

Step Four: Phone Calls

If your business model permits, all prospects should receive regular phone calls to touch base and check their status.

Step 5: Online Follow-up

Through Google and Facebook, you can automatically track and follow up with website visitors using banner ads. And come to think of it, that's not the best part...

A final tip is that different people need different amounts of communication. When I tell you to hit your target list over and over again, the reason is that people move at different speeds in life and in business. Some call after just the first time and some others call after the second time and others call after the fifth time, etc.

Me? I'm fast... I see something I want and I go get it. But my husband is a bit more pragmatic. He'll research and discuss for a while before purchasing.

A lead is anyone that saw your ad and had some level of interest. You can't possibly know what level of interest they had. So you have to assume it is a low level. It is your job as a marketer to warm those leads up over time until they eventually close. I have literally kept the same businesses on my prospect list from the time they got on it until now. A few weeks ago, we sold a campaign to a lovely naturopathic physician that has been in my database since 2005. After a couple of years, we only promote to prospects a few times per year, but we never give up on them.

Now, with those who have called in right away, you may have closes that are slam dunks, but others operate differently when it comes to closing. So don't just waste those leads. Consistently put out your communication in the same way you did with your initial mailings, but with a more personalized message. You'll be glad you did.

26

REVIEWS - HOW TO GET THE GOOD ONES

As the situation stands at the time of writing this, good or bad online reviews can literally make or break someone's decision to reach out to your company or not. I doubt I need to even write that. But it needs to be addressed regardless.

I have known business owners who are petrified of bad reviews. Been there, felt that. Understood. Everyone gets them.

The trick — and your task — is to get an overwhelmingly greater number of 5-star reviews than 1-star reviews. This is honestly not that hard to do. Case in point — at my company, we received over 500 reviews in one year alone after finally devoting to it the attention it deserves. In this chapter, I'll share just how we accomplished that!

Yelp is a problem. Their algorithm (which is a pre-programmed system that dictates how they automatically treat your business) is so unfair. I have a Yelp ad following me around on Facebook, and all the comments are from business owners calling out their unfair business practices. You cannot ask for reviews. If the algorithm thinks too many reviews are coming in at once, it will suppress those reviews to the *"not recommended"* section, so they don't show up on your main Yelp page. The way to combat this is to work on your Google reviews, your BBB (Better Business Bureau) reviews and any and all review sites you can get your hands on: Houzz, Angie's List, Thumbtack, etc.

The system we use is this:
When a customer of ours says something positive to a team member about the service they received or the results of their campaign, we have that team member politely ask the client if they wouldn't mind writing a review. The team member sends them a link to make this easy on them. They also throw in there, *"We play a game here to see who gets the most, so it would really mean a lot to me."* Then we send a link generated by Podium — this has done wonders for us.

podium.com

In 21 years, we had about 320 Google reviews with a 3.6-star rating. Why? Because when people are mad, they are way more likely to go online and spew than if they're satisfied. With the new system in place for two years, we are at 931 reviews with a 4.7-star average rating after 23 total years. We have far more reviews than any of our competitors.

There are many competitors to Podium. Podium costs us about $300/month, $3,600/year. It seems like a lot, but I'm sure we bank way more business because of them. If that's too pricey for your business, you can check out alternatives to Podium, like Trust Pilot, Gather Up, and various others.

If you don't already have a review system in place, there is no better time to start than now. Google *"PostcardMania Clearwater FL reviews"* and see the first page. We work on this proactively. You can too.

27

ALL TOGETHER NOW!
LET'S RECAP!

___

That's it! You have the tools you need to implement (and maintain!) a successful postcard campaign. Enjoy a few moments of self-congratulatory high-fives.

Alright, now get to work growing your business!

Here are some refreshers to guide your way.

1. **Target Your Market**

   Remember, your marketing will produce the best results for the lowest cost when you target prospects who are already interested in what you offer. Who needs your product or service? Targeting answers this question effectively and factually. So always define your market first!

2. **Create a "*Unique Selling Proposition*" for Your Business**

   A Unique Selling Proposition, or USP, is a statement of what
   is different about your company and its products. Your USP
   quickly and succinctly gives people the reason they should do
   business with you. It amplifies the benefit of doing business
   with you and your company. Create your own USP and put it
   on all your promotional materials, invoices, shipping labels,
   etc. Use it to communicate the benefit of doing business with
   you and why you are better than any of your competitors.

3. **Create and Maintain a Database of Prospect and Customer
   Information**

   Remember, most people who receive a postcard from you
   won't contact you the first time they receive one. But once
   they do contact you, you must create and maintain a database
   which allows you to follow up with them until they close. Fifty
   percent or more of sales come as a result of following up with
   people who were previously contacted, but didn't buy right
   away.

4. **Always Include a Call to Action and an Offer**

   Make sure you ask your prospects and customers to DO
   something when they receive your postcard. By offering
   them something you know they are likely to want and giving
   them a smooth path to respond, you are making it easy and
   desirable for them to respond. You have to TELL THEM WHAT
   TO DO. "*Call NOW*" or "*Visit our website TODAY*" are a couple of
   examples of a call to action.

5. **Commit to Consistent Communication Across Several Channels**

   I said it before — postcards are your differentiator. They set you apart from your competition (who are, mostly likely, only advertising online) by making a more meaningful and lasting impression on your target market. That said, postcards alone are not going to be as effective as postcards plus coordinated digital ads, plus follow up, plus doing all of that consistently.

6. **Take Away the Fear of Loss**

   People don't want to be fooled, plain and simple. They have been disappointed too many times by being sold one thing and getting another. A guarantee or warranty is a good way to reduce or eliminate the customers' risk of getting something other than what they bargained for. Guarantees and warranties increase response and sales by reducing customer risk. Another way to reduce fear is to increase the trust and credibility people feel for your business. You can do this by adding photos of you or your team or business to your marketing materials and website, and by communicating with your target market consistently, which shows longevity and legitimacy.

7. **Follow Up, Follow Up, Follow Up**

   Getting new customers is more expensive than selling to existing ones. By regularly following up with your customers and prospects, you can expand your business efficiently and easily. When I say *"older leads,"* I mean anything not from the current day — that's right — yesterday's leads.

   Let me reiterate this. This prospect was interested enough to call. Providing your receptionist was friendly and inviting, you've now got a really good lead there. That lead is more likely to call you again. Your repeat mailings, emails and online ads gain you credibility, but the right offer will bring the dough.

8. **Test Your Postcard Promotions**

   Track the effectiveness of your postcard mailings. How many people responded to your mailing? What dollar amount of sales resulted from those responses? Keep a spreadsheet on this. Monitor it. Tally it and utilize the results to tweak your campaign.

IMPORTANT!

Don't forget to go to Chapter 21: How Much to Mail to figure out where to start your mailing and how much you need to make to turn a profit!

SECTION 5
DIFFERENT INDUSTRIES AND WHAT WORKS FOR THEM

28

POSTCARD CASE STUDIES

Knowledge comes from a wide array of sectors: books, magazines, seminars, classrooms and *The School of Hard Knocks.*

We learn from others, from ourselves, from mentors, from coaches, from colleagues and competitors; if we are receptive to knowledge, they all become our teachers.

In this chapter, I have highlighted case studies of a few of our clients. PostcardMania has created direct mail marketing campaigns for over 102,000 clients in over 350 different industries. If you don't see your industry in this chapter, you can view hundreds more case studies at postcardmania.com/case-studies.

Read all the case studies anyway — sometimes the best idea comes from learning what others are doing outside your own industry. And if you'd like more information on how we have succeeded in helping other businesses in your particular industry, just email us at info@postcardmania.com. Type in the subject line: *"Case Study Request."*

Ziptron Energy

Industry
Fuel Distributor Franchise

Problem Trying to Solve
Ziptron Energy was looking for a way to recruit more independent gas stations to become part of their Mr. Zip franchise. Since this side of the business is focused on Business-2-Business (B2B) sales, Ziptron turned to direct mail to reach their exact target market with an SIC mailing list. (See Chapter 11 for a quick refresher on these lists if needed.)

The Campaign

Ziptron Energy chose a design that features an illuminated gas station, immediately signaling the postcard's relevance to the recipient's business. The strong headline immediately helped recipients recognize the benefits of becoming part of the Ziptron franchise — an instantly recognizable brand that will set them apart from competitors.

Mailing Lists

Ziptron Energy mailed their postcards to a single specialized mailing list over the course of 4 months (with 3 more months of mailings planned). They targeted independent gas stations in Tennessee and omitted franchises that had already bought into another brand. The precision of their list — targeting business owners that would be virtually impossible to reach through digital means alone — along with repetition contributed to their campaign's success.

Results

This campaign generated 8 responses and Ziptron Energy converted 4 of these. They average about $20,000 a sale, meaning they generated around $80,000 in revenue! They only spent $1,759.20 on this campaign so far, so the current return on investment is 4,448% — a number that will continue to climb as they complete their campaign.

Good Hope Land and Timber Management

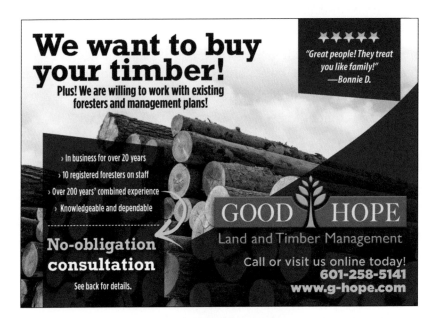

Industry

Land and Forestry Management

Problem Trying to Solve

Good Hope Land and Timber Management specialize in timber purchasing, harvesting and merchandising using sustainable forestry practices. Timber owners and harvesters are an extremely niche group of people, so Good Hope needed to find a targeted way to reach them. That's where direct mail came in.

The Campaign

Their postcard design included a clear headline highlighting their specialty, the benefits of working with them, and a 5-star review from a former client that established credibility. To further maximize their campaign's results, Good Hope ran a direct mail campaign integrated with online marketing, like I outlined in Chapter 19. Their postcards were bundled with ads on Google, Instagram, YouTube, Gmail, and Facebook via our Everywhere Small Business® package. The digital ads coordinated with their postcard design above and helped increase their exposure — and therefore the overall impression they make on their target market.

Mailing Schedule

Good Hope's mailing schedule helped bring in a steady flow of business for them. They mailed between 10,000-13,000 postcards each month for 8 months; this consistency helped ensure timber owners would take notice of their message.

Results

So far, Good Hope has received 493 calls that tracked back to their postcard directly (using the call tracking number that comes free with Everywhere Small Business). They converted about 10% of those responses to sales, which is about 50 new customers! Good Hope Land and Timber Management reported being incredibly happy with the campaign response.

Steve Austin Music

Industry
Performing Musician

Problem Trying to Solve
Steve Austin is a Tennessee-based musician who tours the Southeast annually, showcasing his bluegrass-style music. He was looking for a better way to generate more bookings, so my team helped him come up with a campaign that would keep his schedule full.

The Campaign
Steve's postcard design focused on the unique qualities of his performances and what sets him apart from other musicians. The overall design kept things simple, and the copy detailed the Steve Austin experience. It also contained a limited-time offer that featured the recipient's name on his tour shirt with a booking.

He mailed to a list of a diverse range of businesses likely to host live music events, such as nursing homes, youth organizations, and restaurants. He sent out 1,000 postcards just twice when we spoke to him about his results.

Results
Steve booked 6 in-person shows after just two mailings, with more planned. Each booking earns him about $250 up front, so that is a total of $1,500 generated! And that doesn't include tips he'll make that day or the fact that many of his clients book year after year, resulting in a higher lifetime value of each booking.

Premier Softwash Solutions

Industry

Residential Cleaning

Problem Trying to Solve

Premier Softwash Solutions is an eco-friendly roof and housing exterior cleaning business located just outside of Orlando, FL. They were looking for an effective way to reach homeowners in a specific residential area, so we helped them with postcards.

The Campaign

To grab extra attention, they opted to send out 4" x 9" flyers in the mail. These aren't your typical postcard size or shape, which makes them difficult to ignore.

The design featured:
- A clear and direct headline
- REAL before and after photos that create credibility
- Informative copy explaining the benefits of their unique eco-friendly cleaning process

Mailing List

They went with an Every Door Direct Mail campaign, which targets every house along a mail carrier route in the Orlando area near their business. This saved them a ton on postage and made the most sense since everyone can use their services; there's no need for any micro-targeting.

Results

This campaign generated between 150-200 responses. They told us they typically close about 95% of their leads and the average job runs about $650. That means they would have generated over $100,000!

Results

Premier Softwash Solutions only spent $1,486 on their campaign — that makes their return on investment 6,629%!

Aldine Mail Route Animal Hospital

Industry

Veterinarian

Problem Trying to Solve

This animal hospital located in Houston, TX wanted to increase their new patient numbers in a big way. So, they called us for help to oversee a game-changing, year-long campaign that included mailing postcards and running coordinated Google and Facebook ads using our Everywhere Small Business® product.

The Campaign

We designed an animal service campaign for Aldine Mail Route Animal Hospital — plus matching online Google and Facebook ads — that positioned them as an all-in-one pet services provider.

They offer grooming, health services, surgery and boarding; everything a pet needs to stay happy and healthy.

The design worked really well for this campaign for several reasons:

- The cute photos of dogs and cats immediately grabbed their attention, especially the animal lovers.
- The coupons conveyed a lot of value and immediately let them know that they offer a number of services under one roof.
- They chose to include a map on the back of the card — I love this because they're a local service that targeted nearby homes, so proximity is definitely a benefit.

They mailed consistently too — 5,000 postcards a month for 12 months, saturating the area around their practice with an Every Door Direct Mail mailing list. I love that they committed to a full year of marketing, and it paid off.

Results

Aldine Mail Route Animal Hospital brought in around 1,000 new animal patients that year, and they attribute that success to this campaign. They also increased revenue by 30% over the previous year!

Angel's Pool Service

Industry
Pool Service

Problem Trying to Solve
Angel's Pool Service, located in the small town of Reisterstown, MD, wanted to capitalize on the upcoming pool-opening season and came to us for ideas.

The Campaign
We helped them build a hyper-specific campaign with the goal of creating a revenue spike by only focusing on their pool opening service.

Since every one of their previous clients would need help opening their pools, we decided it was best to start by targeting a list of their previous customers.

A huge contributing factor for this campaign's success was its timing. They sent out a single mailing of just 2,616 postcards at the end of March, right when people in Maryland start to think about using their pools again.

Results
Angel's Pool Service estimates they received 800 responses from this campaign. They converted about 75% of those responses, which generated an estimated $350,000 in revenue. They only spent $1,320 on the campaign, resulting in a MASSIVE return on their investment of 26,415%!

A Solid Reputation With Visible Results.

$150 OFF Any Paint Job Over $1,500! With this card. Offer expires 30 days from mailing date.

CALL NOW FOR MORE INFO!
www.CCsPaintingTN.com | 865-455-4460

Residential & Commercial | Interior & Exterior | Staining | Power Washing
Drywall | Carpentry | Color Consulting & much more!

We Care For Every Detail.

Residential Painting: Interior and Exterior, Limewash Paint, Recote Paint, Wallpaper Removal, Textured Walls and Ceilings, Cabinets, Deck and Fence Staining

Additional Services:

Carpentry: Installation, Repairs, or Replacements

- Rotten wood
- Wood siding
- Trim and baseboard
- Doors

Drywall: Hang Up-Tape-Skim

- Repair cracks, nail pops, nail holes
- Patch holes
- Removal of ceiling or wall texture
- Wall and ceiling texture (popcorn, knock down, stamp, etc.)

For more information on other services provided, please give us a call!
www.CCsPaintingTN.com | 865-455-4460

Pressure Washing | Window Glazing | Deck Sealing | Epoxy Floors | Tile Installation | Color Consultation

232

CC's Painting

Industry
Residential Painter and Cleaner

Problem Trying to Solve
CC's Painting is a family-operated company offering a variety of residential home services. They wanted to reach more homeowners in the Tampa Bay, FL area and solidify their local brand.

The Campaign
To create a presence in their area, they started an Everywhere Small Business® campaign that included targeted postcards alongside matching digital ads on Google, Facebook, and Instagram.

CC's Painting opted for seasonal mailings. Every 3–4 months, they mailed a single drop of around 12,000 postcards, with additional ongoing exposure across Facebook, Instagram, and Google between mailings.

Results
On average, for every 40-50 calls they get from the postcards, they land about 15 jobs!

Country Farms

Industry

Grocer

Problem Trying to Solve

Country Farms is a local market in Edmonds, WA featuring seasonal produce. It's a tough task to compete with the big, national grocery chains, so they came to us to devise a campaign that would boost their bottom line and make them more competitive than the big guys.

The Campaign

They decided on a direct mail marketing campaign bundled with Google, Instagram and Facebook advertising in our Everywhere Small Business® package. They targeted nearby residents with an Every Door Direct Mail mailing list to saturate the area and save on postage. Everyone's gotta eat, right?

Their design used bright and engaging backgrounds of fresh produce to get the attention of prospects. In bright red, recipients immediately saw the 10% off coupon that this postcard offers. The back used a small paragraph to talk about the benefits of buying locally and provided a map so recipients could see just how close their location is.

Results

Country Farms said that over 150 coupons were redeemed! This might not even be all of the results, as many recipients may have come in and not spent enough money to use the coupon. In addition, they also saw a major increase in traffic to their website.

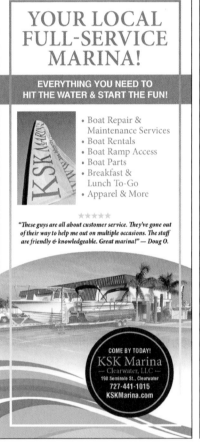

KSK Marina Clearwater

Industry

Full-Service Marina

Problem Trying to Solve

KSK Marina Clearwater wanted a way to promote their services that would expand their customer base. We worked with them to develop a structured marketing campaign that targeted a very specific niche — high-end home and boat owners.

The Campaign

Given the specific goals KSK Marina Clearwater set for their marketing campaign, we decided to target a very distinct group of homes in the area — a resident-occupant list of homeowners along Clearwater Beach with a median home market value of $200,000. This specificity helped ensure that each recipient owned a boat themselves or had enough disposable income to afford renting a boat from the marina. They decided to mail a 4" x 9" flier instead of a traditionally sized postcard to make sure their message stood out in the mail stack. Their design featured a cool color scheme and pictures of their facility with parked boats just waiting to be driven out to sea. Their five-star review built credibility and their map let recipients know immediately that they're local.

Results

KSK Marina Clearwater received 9 new life-long customers! Of those new customers, 8 of them posted reviews and referred friends as well, and they're still getting calls to this day. The cost of their services averages $2,000, so they've made an estimated $18,000 off this campaign!

Rose Wang Dentistry

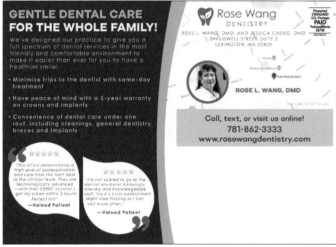

Industry

Dental

Problem Trying to Solve

Rose Wang Dentistry in Lexington, MA has a lot to offer new and current patients. But breaking through the noise and reaching prospects in their area isn't easy — so they turned to postcards for a more direct approach.

The Campaign

After consulting with our team, the dentists at Rose Wang Dentistry decided our Everywhere Dental marketing package offered the best chance for success in their market, since it's a fully integrated service designed exclusively for those in the dental field.

Everywhere Dental consists of three tactics in one convenient package:
- A direct mail campaign to generate lots of quality leads and web traffic
- Digital ads matching your postcard design on Google, Facebook, Instagram, YouTube, and Gmail
- And the real kicker — it includes phone call analysis and scoring. This means a well-trained dental marketing professional personally reviews, analyzes, and rates each one of their tracked phone calls.

Rose Wang Dentistry mailed postcards to 9,000 residents living near their practice via an Every Door Direct Mail list. Using Everywhere Dental's built-in tracking, they could tell exactly who was calling off the postcard and how many people followed the online ads back to their website.

Results

According to Rose Wang Dentistry, they gained an estimated 128 new patients from the postcards. The average lifetime value of their patients is about 2 years with each spending a minimum of $250 per year! That's an estimated revenue of $64,000 over 2 years!

Latimore Group

Industry

Real Estate

Problem Trying to Solve

LaToya Latimore is the owner and business mind behind the Latimore Group real estate agency located in Blythewood, SC. She wanted to run a postcard campaign to get people talking about her services and reached out to us to get a direct mail campaign started.

The Campaign

LaToya Latimore left no marketing stone unturned with her campaign — she opted for our Everywhere Small Business® Platinum, which is an upgrade from the already-efficient Everywhere Small Business.

Everywhere Small Business® Platinum comes with:
- A lead-generating direct mail campaign
- Mail tracking that tells you when your cards will hit
- Call tracking to track and record all calls that come off the campaign
- Ads on Google, Facebook, and Instagram
- The Platinum upgrade — ads on Gmail and YouTube

Latimore Group targeted a mailing list of homeowners more likely to sell their homes within the next 12 months. They also targeted homes in 5 specific zip codes where LaToya Latimore was looking to grow her presence as the go-to real estate agent for the area.

Results

At the time of this writing, her campaign is still active and they've already acquired 4 listings that have closed, generating them $30,000 in revenue!

KEEP YOUR HOME
PEST-FREE
THIS SUMMER WITH OUR
PREVENTION SERVICES

LIMITED TIME SPRING OFFER

$50 OFF
YOUR NEXT SERVICE

See back for details.

DUNGENESS
PEST CONTROL

"Top-notch group. Great from every aspect. From the first phone call it's been easy and everyone is nice and made me feel like it's not a problem because they can get the job done. Kati came for my service call and she is just awesome and I know that after she's through there won't be a rodent or ant that dares to enter my

Call or visit us online!
360-809-1630
www.dungenesspestcontrol.com

KEEP YOUR HOME PEST FREE THIS SUMMER WITH OUR PREVENTION SERVICES

From wasps and ants to rodents and spiders, we have the equipment and skilled crew to ensure no pest is left behind. Our customized service protects your home & yard from uninvited guests while protecting your family and pets.

- Save money with affordable prices
- Enjoy a pest-free home
- Work with a dedicated, professional team

DUNGENESS
PEST CONTROL
1328 E. 1st St.
Port Angeles, WA 98362-4606

Presorted
STANDARD
U.S. Postage
PAID
PostcardMania
33730
D0064977

Call us today to schedule your service!
360-809-1630
www.dungenesspestcontrol.com

Map Data ©2021 Google

Dungeness Pest Control

Industry

Pest Control

Problem Trying to Solve

Dungeness Pest Control is located in Port Angeles, WA. They were looking for a creative way to let nearby residents know they can help keep pests out of their home in the summer months, so they contacted PostcardMania for help.

The Campaign

Their postcard design was appealing and professional, with a headline that immediately touched on a main point for many: incoming summer months means incoming bugs. Yowsa!

They decided on a direct mail marketing campaign that blanketed homes along carrier routes near their business's location with postcards.

Since pests don't discriminate, everyone can use their services. They sent out 40,000 postcards to an Every Door Direct Mail (EDDM) list and mailed out in May and June, which is the beginning of pest season.

Results

Dungeness Pest Control had 125 people redeem their coupon, generating $37,000!

Jill Wedeles Allstate Insurance Agency

Industry

Insurance

Problem Trying to Solve

Jill Wedeles is an Allstate Insurance agent located in Fort Myers, FL. She was looking for a better way to introduce local condo owners to her insurance policies, which cover second homes and their various uses (such as a long-term, short-term, or seasonal rentals), so she reached out to PostcardMania for ideas. She wanted a marketing strategy that would handle a bulk of her promotion automatically (and effectively). In other words, she wanted something that would be *"set it and forget it."*

The Campaign

For the lead generation portion of the campaign, my designers put together a postcard design that used a bright contrasting color scheme to help the card (and message!) stand out in a cluttered mailbox.

Once prospects went to her website, the automated follow-up portion of the campaign kicked in. Prospects who visited the website were automatically tracked and shown follow-up banner ads after they left the site. The ads matched the design of the postcard, even using the same images. So it was an automatic (and super affordable) way to increase repetition and exposure — two must-have elements for successful marketing.

Results

She received 35 calls, 1,211 clicks on her online follow-up ads and 143,901 total online ad impressions (number of times the ad was seen).

The bottom line? Jill Wedeles Allstate Insurance Co brought in 20-30 new insurance policies from the postcard. She estimates these policies will generate approximately $10,000 a month! That's an immediate ROI of 3,494% that will continue to grow exponentially going forward.

Swedish Auto Service

Industry
Automotive Repair

Problem Trying to Solve
This client, a Texas foreign car repair specialist, felt like they had more room to grow. Due to the expensive nature of their services, they wanted to nail down some more consistent customers with an advertising campaign, so they came to PostcardMania for ideas.

The Campaign
After weighing the options, Swedish Auto Service decided to go with a regularly scheduled Everywhere Small Business® campaign that bundled direct mail with Google, Instagram and Facebook ads.

As for the postcard's design, they went with a sleek design featuring sparkling foreign vehicles. Since they were looking to acquire more regular customers, they went with an oil change deal, which isn't that big of a financial commitment and is a good way to build trust and rapport.

The mailing lists targeted 2010-2017 BMW, Mercedes and Volvo owners in a 5-mile radius around their business. They ran 5 separate campaigns, each with 2 mailings per month, over the course of a year.

Results
Swedish Auto Service generates about 20-30 new customers on average, with each individual marketing campaign. The lifetime value of each client is typically around $2,000-$3,000!

The Wyatt Group

Industry

Real Estate Investment

Problem Trying to Solve

The Wyatt Group is a real estate investment company that was looking to acquire more properties, specifically from absentee homeowners (meaning the homeowner's primary residence is somewhere other than the property). Located in Atlanta, GA, The Wyatt Group needed a marketing strategy that could offer excellent results and the ability to reach their specific audience.

The Campaign

For the lead generation portion of the campaign, my designers put together a postcard design that did an excellent job of immediately conveying their core marketing message: sell your home quickly. Their postcard featured a contrasting blue and orange, which grabbed the recipient's attention.

One primary reason for this campaign's success was the specificity of their mailing list. The Wyatt Group provided their own mailing list with the following specs, which delineate a type of consumer likely to be receptive to their messaging:

- Absentee homeowners that have owned the property for 10+ years
- Homes at least 1,000+ square feet containing 3-4 beds and 2 baths in the metro Atlanta area with equity between 1%-49%
- Single- and multi-family rentals with a purchase price between $10,000-$75,000

We delivered 15,000 postcards total to this list, split into 6 smaller mailings of 2,500. Selling a large asset like real estate isn't a decision people come to lightly — it requires the kind of repetition The Wyatt Group offered in order to build trust and legitimacy with their target market. So, did it work?

Results

The Wyatt Group had already closed on 2 listings when we did the initial follow-up, which generated $22,000 in revenue. A great result that immediately more than doubled their initial campaign investment!

Hudson Greene Market

Industry
Grocer

Problem Trying to Solve
Hudson Greene Market is an organic, health-focused grocer located in the heart of Jersey City, NJ. They contact us with a desire to increase their clientele and boost revenue

The Campaign
Hudson Greene Market opted to target nearby residents with an Everywhere Small Business® (ESB) campaign, which combined direct mail postcards with matching digital ads on Google, Facebook and Instagram.

The design of their postcard was clean and simple. It immediately conveyed freshness, brightness and variety — something most people look for in a grocer. The large coupons on the back of their postcard offered real value and encouraged people to hold on to this postcard. Maybe you stick it on the fridge, put it on the counter or tuck it into a purse or bag — which is a great way to earn a ton of repeat impressions until it's finally shopping day.

Where to purchase groceries is a decision that people take much more lightly than whether they want to sell their home. So they were able to get away with a single mailing of 6,000 cards to nearby residents. But remember — with Everywhere Small Business, interested recipients were still seeing digital ads for 3 more months following that mailing. These digital reminders are an excellent way to continue following up with recipients and building trust and credibility.

Results
The digital side of their campaign totaled 182,500 impressions and 1,491 clicks on their digital ads. As for the postcards, Hudson Greene Market counted 50 coupons redeemed in store, generating over $12,000 in income. This is an immediate ROI of 184%!

This ROI doesn't even include repeat shoppers, who, now that they've gone there and bought something, will likely return again and again, boosting their ROI higher and higher over time. Remember the lesson from Chapter 7? It's much harder to convince someone to be your customer the first time. Repeat orders are MUCH easier to attain than new ones.

American Land Ventures

Industry

Real Estate

Problem Trying to Solve

American Land Ventures is a real estate developer that runs Altaire Apartments, a brand new luxury multi-family rental property in Orlando, FL. Their management team wanted to introduce their newly finished property to the area, so they decided to host an open house event and get the word out to nearby renters through direct mail.

The Campaign

My team worked with American Land Ventures to target people most likely to sign a lease at a luxury apartment complex — renters already living in competing apartment complexes nearby. This audience had already demonstrated a few key things: they like the area; they're renters, not homeowners; and they can afford a higher monthly rent.

Since their open house is a free, one-time event, renters aren't likely to need much convincing to attend. A one-time drop of 5,000 postcards in February, prior to their open house, was enough to move the needle on this campaign and generate a result.

Results

American Land Ventures landed 37 new leases from people who attended the event, making it a massive success. The average number of new leases a month is 25, and they received 37 in just 2 weeks. They expect to receive an annual income of $69,000 from these new leases! They only spent $3,363.05 on this campaign, resulting in a 1,952% return on their investment!! And that's just the first year's return and doesn't take multi-year residencies into account.

SECTION 6
GLOSSARY

29

KEY MARKETING TERMS DEFINED

In this manual, I've tried to include only those industry buzzwords I felt would be helpful to you. As a parting gift, and in recognition of the fact that you are soon to hold an honorary degree with PostcardMania (which makes you an honorary *"maniac"*), I wanted to share some more technical terms with you that you might come across as you delve further into direct mail marketing's most successful secret. Enjoy:

Advertising
Advertising is paid communication through a non-personal medium in which the sponsor is identified and the message is controlled (www.wikipedia.com).

Affiliate Program

An online marketing strategy that involves revenue sharing between online advertisers/merchants and online publishers/salespeople. Compensation is typically awarded based on performance measures such as sales, clicks, registrations or a combination of factors. (www.marketingpower.com)

B2B

Business to Business — a company that sells goods or services to businesses.

B2C

Business to Consumer — a company that sells goods or services to consumers.

Banner Ads

A web banner or banner ad is a form of advertising online. This form of online advertising entails embedding an advertisement into a web page. It is intended to attract traffic to a website by linking them to the website of the advertiser (wikipedia.com).

Benefits

Something that is advantageous or good; an advantage (dictionary.com).

Bio

An account of somebody's life written or produced by another person, e.g. as a book, movie or television program [Encarta].

Blog

A blog is a user-generated website where entries are made in a journal style and displayed in a reverse chronological order.

Blogs often provide commentary or news on a particular subject, such as food, politics, or local news; some function as more personal online diaries.

A typical blog combines text, images, and links to other blogs, web pages, and other media related to its topic. The ability for readers to leave comments in an interactive format is an important part of most early blogs. Most blogs are primarily textual, although some focus on photographs (photoblog), sketchblog, videos (vlog), or audio (podcasting), and are part of a wider network of social media. The term blog is a portmanteau, or, in other words, a blend of the words web and log (web log). Blog can also be used as a verb, meaning to maintain or add content to a blog (wikipedia.com).

Body
The principal part of a speech or document, minus introduction, conclusion, indexes, etc (dictionary.com).

Branding
In marketing, the use of logos, symbols, or product design to promote consumer awareness of goods and services (dictionary. com).

BRC
Business Reply Card — A pre-addressed postcard that the recipient can mail back to the sender requesting more information about whatever was advertised on the mail piece. Usually a BRC includes a prepaid postcard indicia so the recipient doesn't have to pay postage to send it back.

BRE

Business Reply Envelope — Same as BRC but in envelope form.

Button

A hidden sensitivity that can be manipulated to produce a desired response e.g. *"knows how to push my buttons"* (m-w.com).

Buying Motivation

The forces that have been activated into a state of tension causing the buyer to seek satisfaction of a specific need. Organizational buyers are influenced by both rational appeals (e.g., economic factors such as cost, quality, and service) and emotional appeals (e.g., status, security, and fear).

Call To Action (CTA)

The implicit or explicit suggestion contained in a marketer's content in an advertisement or website copy. Example: *"The call to action said, "Click Here to enter a survey to qualify to win a prize"* (dictionary.com).

Click-through

Term used to measure the number of users who clicked on a specific internet advertisement or link.

Content

The principal substance (as written matter, illustrations, or music) offered by a World Wide Web site. Internet users have evolved an ethos of free content in the internet — Ben Gerson (m-w.com).

Conversion Rate or Hit Rate

The percentage of the desired number of outcomes received by a salesperson relative to the total activity level. For example, it is the number of sales as a percentage of the number of calls. It also is called batting average and conversion rate.

Cookie

A packet of data sent by an internet server to a browser, which is returned by the browser each time it subsequently accesses the same server, used to identify the user or track their access to the server.

Copywriter

Copywriting is the process of writing the words that promote a person, business, opinion, or idea. It may be used as plain text, as a radio or television advertisement, or in a variety of other media. The main purpose of writing this marketing copy, or promotional text, is to persuade the listener or reader to act — to buy a product or subscribe to a certain viewpoint, for instance. Alternatively, copy might also be intended to dissuade a reader from a particular belief or action (wikipedia.com).

Cost Per Click (CPC)

Pay-per-click (PPC) (also called cost per click) is an internet advertising model used to direct traffic to websites, in which advertisers pay the publisher (typically a website owner) when the ad is clicked. It is defined simply as *"the amount spent to get an advertisement clicked."*

CRM

Customer Relationship Management — A discipline in marketing combining database and computer technology with customer service and marketing communications. Customer relationship management (or CRM) seeks to create more meaningful one-on-one communications with the customer by applying customer data (demographic, industry, buying history, etc.) to every communications vehicle. At the simplest level, this would include personalizing email or other communications with customer names. At a more complex level, CRM enables a company to produce a consistent, personalized marketing communication whether the customer sees an ad, visits a website or calls customer service.

Data Mining

The analytical process of finding new and potentially useful knowledge from data. The process includes the use of mathematical tools to find difficult patterns of intelligence (marketingpower.com).

Database Marketing

An approach by which computer database technologies are harnessed to design, create, and manage customer data lists containing information about each customer's characteristics and history of interactions with the company. The lists are used as needed for locating, selecting, targeting, servicing and establishing relationships with customers in order to enhance the long-term value of these customers to the company.
The techniques used for managing lists include: 1. Database manipulation methods such as select and join, 2. Statistical methods for predicting each customer's likelihood of future purchases of specific items based on his/her history of past

purchases, and 3. Measures for computing the lifetime value of a customer on an ongoing basis (marketingpower.com).

Demographic

The study of total size, sex, territorial distribution, age, composition, and other characteristics of human populations; the analysis of changes in the make-up of a population (marketingpower.com).

Direct Mail

The use of the mail delivered by the U.S. Postal Service or other delivery services as an advertising media vehicle (marketingpower.com).

Direct Marketing

1. (retailing definition) A form of nonstore retailing in which customers are exposed to merchandise through an impersonal medium and then purchase the merchandise by telephone or mail. 2. (channels of distribution definition) The total of activities by which the seller, in affecting the exchange of goods and services with the buyer, directs efforts to a target audience using one or more media (direct selling, direct mail, telemarketing, direct-action advertising, catalog selling, cable selling, etc.) for the purpose of soliciting a response by phone, mail, or personal visit from a prospect or customer (marketingpower.com).

Direct Response Advertising

An approach to the advertising message that includes a method of response, such as an address or telephone number, whereby members of the audience can respond directly to the advertiser in order to purchase a product or service offered in the advertising message. Direct response advertising can be conveyed to members of a target market by a wide variety of advertising media, including television, radio, magazines, mail delivery, etc (marketingpower.com).

Dissemination
To scatter or spread widely, as though sowing seed; promulgate extensively; broadcast; disperse: to disseminate information about preventive medicine (dictionary.com).

Domain Name
A unique identifier for an internet site which consists of at least two (but sometimes more) parts separated by periods (e.g., http://www.info-edge.com). Enterprises must register top-level domains with the Web Internet Registry and pay a yearly fee to maintain the registry.

EDDM
Every Door Direct Mail (EDDM) is a direct mail service offered by USPS®. With EDDM, you select neighborhoods (carrier routes) in which you would like USPS to deliver a mailpiece to every address or delivery point within the selected routes.

ESB
Everywhere Small Business® (ESB) is an automatic system that saves you countless hours and maximizes your marketing impact beyond anything else you've tried. When you add Everywhere Small Business® to your direct mail campaign, your targeted prospects see your ads on Google, Facebook, Instagram, Youtube and Gmail automatically. Plus, the results of your campaign are tracked in one easy-to-use dashboard which also

records any phone calls you receive so that you can ensure your reception team is handling your leads properly.

Email Marketing

Email marketing is a form of direct marketing which uses electronic mail as a means of communicating commercial or fundraising messages to an audience. In its broadest sense, every email sent to a potential or current customer could be considered email marketing. However, the term is usually used to refer to:

Sending emails with the purpose of enhancing the relationship of a merchant with its current or old customers and to encourage customer loyalty and repeat business.

Sending emails with the purpose of acquiring new customers or convincing old customers to buy something immediately. Adding advertisements in emails sent by other companies to their customers.

Emails that are being sent on the internet. (Email did and does exist outside the internet, Network Email, FIDO etc.) (wikipedia.com).

Features

Something offered to the public or advertised as particularly attractive (m-w.com).

Focus Groups

A focus group is a form of qualitative research in which a group of people are asked about their attitude towards a product, service, concept, advertisement, idea, or packaging. Questions are asked in an interactive group setting where participants are free to talk with other group members.

In the world of marketing, focus groups are an important tool for acquiring feedback regarding new products, as well as various topics. In particular, focus groups allow companies wishing to develop, package, name, or test market a new product, to discuss, view, and/or test the new product before it is made available to the public. This can provide invaluable information about the potential market acceptance of the product (wikipedia.com).

Google Ads
Google Ads is a cost-per-click (CPC) advertising. You pay only when users click on your ad. It has features that allow you to control your costs by setting a daily budget for what you are willing to spend per day. Google Ads sponsored listings are also being shown on Google's partner sites. https://support.google.com/admanager/table/7636513?hl=en

Guerilla Marketing
In The Guerrilla Marketing Handbook, the writer states: *"In order to sell a product or a service, a company must establish a relationship with the customer. It must build trust and rapport. It must understand the customer's needs, and it must provide a product that delivers the promised benefits."*

Headline
The part of the written component of print advertising that is meant to help attract the reader's attention to the ad (marketingpower.com).

HTML (HyperText Markup Language)
A standardized system for tagging text files to achieve font, color, graphic, and hyperlink and layout effects on website pages.

Image
The consumer perception of a product, institution, brand, business, or person that may or may not correspond with *"reality"* or *"actuality."* For marketing purposes the *"image of what is"* may be more important than *"what actually is"* (marketingpower. com).

Internet Marketing
Internet marketing is the use of the internet to advertise and sell goods and services. Internet Marketing includes pay-per-click advertising, banner ads, email marketing, affiliate marketing, interactive advertising, search engine marketing (including search engine optimization), blog marketing, article marketing, and blogging (wikipedia.com).

Interactive Advertising
The use of interactive media to promote and/or influence the buying decisions of the consumer in an online and offline environment. Interactive advertising can utilize media such as the internet, social media, interactive television, mobile devices, as well as kiosk-based terminals.

Interactive advertising affords the marketer the ability to engage the consumer in a direct and personal way, enabling a sophisticated and dimensional dialogue, which can affect a potential customer's buying decisions particularly in an e-commerce environment.

Perhaps one of the most effective implementations of interactive advertising is so-called viral marketing. This technique uses images, texts, web links, Flash animations, audio/video clips etc., passed from user to user chain letter-style, via email. A notable example of this is the Subservient Chicken, a campaign by Burger King to promote their new line of chicken sandwiches and the *"Have It Your Way"* campaign (wikipedia.com).

Keywords
A word or phrase (called a keyword phrase) that is used to help index content on web pages so search engines such as Google can better categorize them and deliver those pages appropriately when people conduct searches.

Landing Page
In online marketing, a landing page is a specific web page that a visitor ultimately reaches after clicking a link or advertisement. Often, this page showcases content that is an extension of the link or ad, or the page is optimized for a specific keyword term or phrase to attract search engines.

A landing page will often be customized in PPC campaigns as a way to both monitor the effectiveness of paid ads as well as a way to supply copy, images, or other content that is specifically targeted to the advertisement. By adding parameters to the linking URL, marketers can compare ad effectiveness based on relative click-through rates (wikipedia.com).

Lead Generation
Lead generation is a marketing term that refers to the manufacture of connections between well-matched consumers and target corporate vendors. There are several methods used in

marketing lead generation:

- Advertising
- Trade Shows
- Publicity and Public Relations
- Product Literature
- Spam (dubiously)
- (wikipedia.com)

Link Popularity

A measure of the quantity and quality of sites that link to your site. Often used as one of the criteria to determine rank on search engines (marketingpower.com).

Market

A specific group of people who have needs to satisfy and the ability to pay (purchasing power).

Market Life Cycle

The period of time that a substantial segment of the buying public is interested in purchasing a given product or service.

Market Potential

The maximum achievable combined sales volume for all sellers of a specific product during a specific time period, in a specific market (marketingpower.com).

Market Research

Market research is the process of systematic gathering, recording and analyzing of data about customers, competitors and the market. Market research can help create a business plan, launch a new product or service, fine tune existing products and services, expand into new markets, etc. It can be used to determine which portion of the population will purchase the product/service, based on variables like age, gender, location and income level. It can be found out what market characteristics your target market has. With market research, companies can learn more about current and potential customers (wikipedia.com).

Market Segmentation
Market segmentation is the process in marketing of dividing a market into distinct subsets (segments) that behave in the same way or have similar needs. Because each segment is fairly homogeneous in their needs and attitudes, they are likely to respond similarly to a given marketing strategy. That is, they are likely to have similar feelings and ideas about a marketing mix comprised of a given product or service, sold at a given price, distributed in a certain way, and promoted in a certain way (wikipedia.com).

Market Share
The percentage of the total sales (from all sources) of a service or product represented by the sales made by your enterprise. i.e., your sales, divided by total sales (marketingpower.com).

Marketing
The process or technique of promoting, selling, and distributing a product or service (m-w.com).

Marketing Strategy
A statement (implicit or explicit) of how a brand or product line will achieve its objectives. The strategy provides decisions and direction regarding variables such as the segmentation of the market, identification of the target market, positioning, marketing mix elements, and expenditures. A marketing

strategy is usually an integral part of a business strategy that provides broad direction to all functions (<u>marketingpower.com</u>).

Mass Media

Mass media is a term used to denote, as a class, that section of the media specifically conceived and designed to reach a very large audience, such as the population of a state. It was coined in the 1920s with the advent of nationwide radio networks, mass-circulation newspapers and magazines, although mass media was present centuries before the term became common (<u>wikipedia.com</u>).

Media Advisory

A media advisory is an abbreviated form of alerting the media when an event is about to happen, but there is not a lot of time before it occurs. Only pertinent data — but not too much, is relevant in this advisory: what, when, where and who to meet there.

Meta Tags

HTML coding used to describe various features of a web page (<u>marketingpower.com</u>).

News Release

Same as a press release — these words are interchangeable. See press release.

Opinion Leader

The opinion leader is the agent who is an active media user and who interprets the meaning of media messages or content for lower-end media users. Typically the opinion leader is held in high esteem by those that accept their opinions. Opinion leadership tends to be subject specific, that is, a person that is an opinion leader in one field may be a follower in another field. An example of an opinion leader in the field of computer technology might be a neighborhood computer service technician. The technician has access to far more information on this topic than the average consumer and has the requisite background to understand the information (wikipedia.com).

Opt In

A program where membership is restricted to users who specifically requested to take part, such as a newsletter (marketingpower.com).

Opt Out

A type of program that assumes inclusion unless stated otherwise. The term also refers to the process of removing one's name from a program (marketingpower.com).

Podcast

A podcast is a media file that is distributed over the internet using syndication feeds for playback on portable media players and personal computers. Like "radio," it can mean both the content and the method of syndication. The latter may also be termed podcasting. The host or author of a podcast is often called a podcaster. The term *"podcast"* is derived from Apple's portable music player, the iPod (wikipedia.com).

Positioning

Positioning is what the advertiser does for the product in the prospect's mind. In other words — the perception of the product or service to the prospect that is developed through ads. 7-Up, the Un-Cola etc.

PPC

Pay-per-click (PPC) is an advertising technique used on websites, advertising networks and search engines.

Advertisers bid on *"keywords"* that they believe their target market (people they think would be interested in their offer) would type in the search bar when they are looking for their type of product or service. For example, if an advertiser sells red widgets, he/she would bid on the keyword *"red widgets,"* hoping a user would type those words in the search bar, see their ad, click on it and buy. These ads are called *"sponsored links"* or *"sponsored ads"* and appear next to and sometimes above the natural or organic results on the page. The advertiser pays only when the user clicks on the ad (wikipedia.com).

Press Release

A news release, press release or press statement is a written or recorded communication directed at members of the news media for the purpose of announcing something claimed as having news value. Typically, it is mailed, faxed, or emailed to assignment editors at newspapers, magazines, radio stations, television stations and/or television networks. Commercial newswire services are also used ,such as Eworldwire, to distribute news releases (wikipedia.com).

Promotion

The act of furthering the growth or development of something; especially: the furtherance of the acceptance and sale of merchandise through advertising, publicity, or discounting (m-w.com).

Public Relations (PR)

Public relations (PR) is the business, organizational, philanthropic, or social function of managing communication between an organization and its audiences. There are many goals to be achieved by the practice of public relations, including education, correcting a mistruth, or building or improving an image (wikipedia.com).

Publicity

Publicity is the deliberate attempt to manage the public's perception of a subject. The subjects of publicity include people (for example, politicians and performing artists), goods and services, organizations of all kinds, and works of art or entertainment.

From a marketing perspective, publicity is one component of promotion. The other elements of the promotional mix are advertising, sales promotion, and personal selling. Promotion is one component of marketing.

Between the client and selected target audiences, publicity is the management of product or brand-related communications between the firm and the general public. It is primarily an informative activity (as opposed to a persuasive one), but its ultimate goal is to promote the client's products, services, or brands (wikipedia.com).

RFM — Recency Frequency Monetary

RFM is a method used for analyzing customer behavior and defining market segments. It is commonly used in database marketing and direct marketing and has received particular attention in retail.

RFM stands for:

Recency — When was the last order?

Frequency — How many orders have they placed with us?

Monetary Value — What is the value of their orders?

(wikipedia.com)

ROI

Return on Investment (ROI), is the ratio of money gained or lost on an investment relative to the amount of money invested (wikipedia). With marketing, it is the ratio of the amount of income you brought in from sales directly from your marketing relative to the amount of money spent on that marketing.

RSS

RSS is a family of web feed formats used to publish frequently updated digital content, such as blogs, news feeds or podcasts.

Users of RSS content use programs called feed readers or aggregators: the user subscribes to a feed by supplying to their reader a link to the feed; the reader can then check the user's subscribed feeds to see if any of those feeds have new content since the last time it checked, and if so, retrieve that content and present it to the user.

The initials "*RSS*" are variously used to refer to the following standards:

Really Simple Syndication (RSS 2.0)

Rich Site Summary (RSS 0.91, RSS 1.0)

RDF Site Summary (RSS 0.9 and 1.0)

(wikipedia).

Sales Copy or Ad Copy
The verbal or written component of advertising messages.

SEO
The process of developing a marketing/technical plan to ensure effective use of search engines as a marketing tool. Typically consists of two elements. On a technical side, SEO refers to ensuring that a website can be indexed properly by the major search engines including keywords, content, and links. On the marketing side, SEO refers to the process of targeting specific keywords where the site should *"win"* in searches. This can be done by modifying a website to score well in the algorithms search engines use to determine rank. Often, SEO programs are a blend of several elements and strategies (wikipedia.com).

Shotgun Approach
A marketing strategy that directs a new product to an entire market, or to the largest segment in it, solely because of its size. Today, this shotgun approach is felt to be almost always inferior to the alternative strategy of targeting smaller segments (wikipedia.com).

Strategic Relationships
An agreement between two or more enterprises to conduct specified business processes in a joint manner. Usually related to technology development and/or marketing and distribution efforts.

Subhead
A part of the written component of print advertising that is designed to guide the reader's attention to specific details about

the advertised item or to help organize issues presented in the body copy.

Survey Monkey
An online survey service which compiles responses. See www.surveymonkey.com.

Target Market
A specific group of customers at which a company aims its products and services.

The 4 P's
Product: The product management and product marketing aspects of marketing deal with the specifications of the actual good or service and how it relates to the end-user's needs and wants.

Pricing: This refers to the process of setting a price for a product, including discounts. The price need not be monetary — it can simply be what is exchanged for the product or service, e.g. time, or attention.

Promotion: This includes advertising, sales promotion, publicity, and personal selling, and refers to the various methods of promoting the product, brand, or company.

Placement: This is distribution and refers to how the product gets to the customer; for example, point of sale placement or retailing. This fourth P has also sometimes been called Place, referring to the channel by which a product or service is sold (e.g. online vs. retail), which geographic region or industry to which segment (young adults, families, business people), etc.

Unique Visitors

A unique visitor is a statistic describing a unit of traffic to a website, counting each visitor only once in the time frame of the report. This statistic is relevant to site publishers and advertisers as a measure of a site's true audience size, equivalent to the term *"reach"* used in other media.

The number of total visitors to a site divided by unique visitors results in the derived statistic *"Average Sessions Per Unique Visitor,"* which tells a publisher how many times each unique visitor came to their site on average in the time frame of the report. Average Sessions Per Unique Visitor is equivalent to *"Frequency"* used in other media.

The Unique Visitors statistic can only be measured accurately in two ways with current technology:
1) by requiring all visitors to log into the site, thereby capturing the identity of each visitor on each visit, or 2) by placing a cookie on each visitor's computer, writing the cookie ID to a database, and checking for the cookie on each visitor's computer each time they visit (wikipedia.com).

USP — Unique Selling Proposition

An approach to developing the advertising message that concentrates on the uniquely differentiating characteristic of the product that is both important to the customer and a unique strength of the advertised products when compared to competing products (marketingpower.com).

Value Added

Value added refers to the additional value created at a particular stage of production or through image and marketing (wikipedia.com).

Vertical Market

A situation in which an industrial product is used by only one or very few industry or trade groups. The market is narrow but deep in the sense that most prospective customers in the industry may need the product or service (marketingpower.com).

Viral Marketing

Viral marketing and viral advertising refer to marketing techniques that use pre-existing social networks to produce increases in brand awareness through self-replicating viral processes, analogous to the spread of pathological and computer viruses. It can often be word-of-mouth delivered and enhanced online; it can harness the network effect of the internet and can be very useful in reaching a large number of people rapidly.

Some of the first recorded offline/online viral campaigns were developed by Tim Nolan of Spent2000.com fame circa 1996. By placing abstract pairings of catch phrases, quotes, song lyrics and image mashups, Mr. Nolan developed a method of creating buzz around a URL-based installation. Phrases like, *"This city isn't safe"* placed alongside a URL created enough curiosity in people's minds to remember a URL and visit again once they were online (wikipedia.com).

Web Browser

A web browser is a software application that enables a user to display and interact with text, images, and other information typically located on a web page, at a website, on the World Wide Web or a local area network. Some of the web browsers available for personal computers include Internet Explorer, Mozilla Firefox, Safari, Netscape, and Opera in order of descending popularity (marketingpower.com).

Webmaster

A webmaster is a person responsible for designing, developing, marketing, or maintaining website(s). The webmaster of a website may also be called a system administrator, the author of a site, or the website administrator (<u>wikipedia.com</u>).